Library and Archives Canada Cataloguing in Publication

Brick, Fred, 1935-
Brick by Brick / by Fred Brick.

ISBN 1-896150-17-9
I. Title.

PS8603.R52B74 2004 C818'.602 C2004-906877-6

CREDITS

Editing	Louise Auger
Design	Dawn Huck
Illustrations	Linda Marchand, Susan Muscovitch and Stuart Brick
Back cover photography	Image 2
Front cover photography	Lisa Brick
Prepress & Printing	Avenue 4 Communications

Special thanks to Cynthia Brick for initiating and assisting with the project throughout.

Canada Council for the Arts Conseil des Arts du Canada

We gratefully acknowledge the support of the Canada Council for the Arts.

Brick by Brick

by Fred Brick

Heartland Associates Inc.
Winnipeg, Canada

Printed in Winnipeg, Canada

More than Fine Furniture

IF YOU'VE BEEN a regular reader of his articles in the *Free Press* on Sunday morning you know that "Fred Brick owns Brick's Fine Furniture". You also know that he owns a very smart and very sarcastic dog called Roxy.

Since 1993, Fred has written nearly 600 articles. Imagine having to write an article every week, week after week, month after month, for more than a decade. As he explains in his introduction, at first Fred wrote about furniture — case goods, accessories, fabrics and colours. But, inevitably, and to his wife's dismay, he began to digress. Inspiration sprang from his everyday world, revealing details about life with his wife at home and at work, with his children and even with Mrs. Dreman, his mother-in-law. His irrepressible sense of humour emerged as self-directed put-downs.

For a while his wife of 44 years, the omniscient Cynthia, delivered the funniest lines, but she was displaced, gradually, by the diva Roxy. Roxy, a people's princess, is a brilliant anthropomorphic invention, a perfect foil for his sometimes curmudgeonly opinions. But oh! Do not fear — Roxy does exist, the latest of a series of pets upon which he has lavished love and attention. Roxy adores him — in a pre-feminist kind of way — and joyfully pants and waves her tail when she sees him or even suspects that he's near. It is clear that Fred and Roxy enjoy a solid relationship.

The son of Philip and Ida Brick, Fred's reminiscences of his parents' fruit and vegetable shop and of the carefree days of his youth, are the source of many of his stories. He has a great sense of humour and a seemingly endless repertoire of jokes. And he loves Manitoba and adores all its seasons, particularly autumn, a preference shared by Roxy, if you throw in dry leaves and a few squirrels. Fred also loves the great outdoors, walking through the park in all kinds of weather, and he spends a great deal of time gardening — outside and in his greenhouse.

Fred is not above using his soapbox to rail against the night or to get even with some salesclerk who irritated him but, generous to a fault, he is a great booster of events such as the Manitoba Marathon. Some of his best articles praise friends, people who worked for Bricks and even competitors in the furniture business. For him there is nothing boring about Winnipeg — he is in tune with the city especially with what he calls the "nord end". Away on some business trip, he eagerly returns home.

Fred and Cynthia started their furniture store on a shoe string some 35 years ago. Fred's childhood coin collection, sold for $1,400, financed the endeavour. Parents of five children, the last of whom were partly raised in the shop, they nurtured their successful company to where it is today. There is a "David and Goliath" quality about Fred. When the business name of their company was threatened a few years ago he took up the challenge armed only with the certitude that he was right. This doggedness is the characteristic that also underpinned his long career as a writer.

Humour, self-deprecation and a love of life — these combine to make his writing timeless. And those of us who have enjoyed his columns over the years are delighted to see a sampling of them gathered here.

Louise Auger
November 2004

Our very own celebrity

GROWING UP IN A FAMILY OF FIVE KIDS we had the privilege of listening to our Dad's stories first-hand. Whether at the dinner table, at bedtime or whenever, Dad would always be happy to share one of his many amusing anecdotes. We grew up thinking that everybody had a similar experience: a father with an endless supply of funny stories and jokes.

We tended to take these stories for granted. And as we got older, we didn't have as much time to listen to our Dad. We had other important things to do, like talking on the phone or hanging out with our friends.

When Dad starting writing his column in the *Free Press*, he found a new outlet for his stories, not to mention a new audience. Many of the stories that made their way into the paper were ones we had heard growing up, but there were also new tales about our family and about Roxy, the dog.

Sometimes we'd read the columns and wonder if anyone else would find these stories as funny as we had. Would people find our family escapades endearing? Would they fall in love with Roxy the way our Dad had? Little did we know the impact his articles would have!

All of a sudden, perfect strangers began to approach us as though they knew us, asking questions about our Dad, our family and, of course, about Roxy. They'd tell us how much they loved Dad's column and how they looked forward to reading it on Sundays.

Dad always enjoyed these encounters. Suddenly, we had a celebrity on our hands. People from all walks of life would whisper in awe: "Is that Fred Brick?" "Is that Roxy?"

You know that your father's well known when Randy Carlyle, captain of the Winnipeg Jets, yells "Hey, Fred!"across Winnipeg Airport and you realize it's your Dad he's calling!

We're sure our father had no idea that his columns would touch such a chord with people. It's certainly true that as his offspring, we had no idea! He wrote the columns as a labor of love, and enjoyed every minute. Now, in this collection of articles, you'll be able to see them all over again and we hope you enjoy reading them this time as much as we have.

And to our Dad, thank you for sharing your wit and your unique writing style. We can't wait to see the next book!

Love always,
Your children and grandchildren
And, of course, Roxy
November 2004

Of writing ... and Roxy

By Fred Brick

BEING AN AVID GARDENER and lover of the outdoors has often impeded my endeavors as a writer. In fact, as I write this, in November, I'm suffering great angst because I haven't yet finished planting my tulips!

My writing career began in a rather unusual way. Besides a few stories here and there, the most consistent writing I'd ever done was letters to my brother Jerry, caused by his abandoning me and moving family and all to Toronto. The fact that he enjoyed my missives gave me heart to venture into other settings, like Letters to the Editor of the *Winnipeg Free Press*. This gave me some fleeting fame ... and my wife heartburn.

About twelve years ago (has it really been that long?), my advertising rep at the *Free Press*, Mr. Ron Delaronde, offered me a space in the paper's Home section if I would write a column on furniture.

I did. The early columns were carefully crafted, pieces designed to be informative. At times they were so much so, I nearly fell asleep writing them. So I discreetly inserted a few columns about life, and found a niche.

I mostly enjoy doing them, except at four in the morning, with a deadline approaching, when I'm staring at a blank computer screen.

To my readers, I have enjoyed your letters, e-mails, phone calls, and talks on the street, in the malls or in the parks immensely. You've made me feel part of your life, as you tell me you feel part of mine. As in one of my favorite airs: "You Raise Me Up".

And if I don't mention my dog Roxy, she'll be impossible to live with. She's truly a wonderful companion, and asks only to go on all and any car rides and morning walks, and to have her meals strictly on time. The parks and woodlands are very special to us. We both love romping through them. She examines every gopher hole and gives the squirrels and wild turkeys a bit of exercise.

Roxy says little, but has somehow taken over the column. One of the most oft heard questions I receive is: "Are you Roxy's Dad?"

I am.

Table of Contents

December 26, 1993

Beware of those cattails

Accessories are a vital part of our indoor decor. Some of the most touching and beautiful items are found in the world of plants — live and not-so-live.

The Christmas tree is a unique expression of the warmth and closeness that permeates this festive season and demands to be the focal point of its area.

Live plants dress up a room as few other items can. Their burst of color and life is marvelous in the dead of winter.

The beautiful poinsettia hybridized into neon-like colorations is the overwhelming Yule favorite while mums, azaleas, Kalanchoe and many more are excellent choices now and throughout the year.

While the beauty of live plants is obvious, the natural beauty of dried native plants can add a subtle enhancement to most settings.

My wife and I were avid campers at one stage and during some of our winter sorties we would trudge through fields and off-roads.

We passed many indigenous dried plants, their pristine beauty breaking through the snow and commanding attention.

We brought home a few bouquets that graced our home (and memories) for the season and even much longer. I hesitate to mention the first time we did this, but my wife won't be happy until I've bared my soul.

We picked a few cattails from a frozen marsh. She asked if they would "shed" when dried. Knowing better, I guffawed. We took them home and arranged them beautifully with some dried millet. Not that long later we came home from work and once again I was right, sort of.

They didn't "kinda shed". They exploded!

We came home to a room surrounded with fluff and if you didn't get irate — like some people — it looked sort of, well, ethereal.

Don't bring home no cattails!

ACCESSORIES au Natural

September 4, 1994

Where shall we sleep tonight, dear?

I rather like the Victorian suite but if you prefer the Oriental, fine.

This is probably not your everyday (or night) discussion with your mate. Nor ours, except in November '86, we had a similar conversation during one of Winnipeg's notorious blizzards, a two-and-a-half day and night affair that would bring most cities to their knees and slowed Winnipeg down a little more than somewhat.

It was a Friday and by early afternoon we knew we had bought a big one. The snowfall increased and the winds were picking up. The radio had constant updates, and your stomach started getting queasy.

We also knew that we could probably make it home if we left shortly. But if anything happened at the building — frozen pipes, broken windows, power outage or any of those good things — how would we get back to them?

We decided to stay. We rarely take holidays and this could be turned into a sort of fun time — no kids, no dog, just each other.

I phoned home and told the kids where mom and dad would be for a couple of days. My wife spoke also, making them promise to keep the house clean and explaining the horrid penalties for civil disobedience.

We did a tour of "the estate," spent some time by the radio and went for supper at the Westin, across the street.

We got out with the help of a shovel and really needed it to get back in.

We did bed down with the Victorian suite one night and a contemporary collection the next — that was the good part.

The bad was that we had no nibbling food. You don't realize how many times you go to your fridge for an apple, cheese, or whatever.

We lasted, almost intact, but I'm pretty sure on that second night if my wife had had her "druthers," she would likely have traded me for a box of Ritz crackers!

BED AND BREAKFAST?

September 25, 1994

Try produce for centrepiece

One of the wondrous things about Manitoba is its clearly defined seasons. Our outside world couldn't be more so. Spring is alive with birds, new growth and the odd late frost. Summer is vibrant with flowers, bugs and the rare early frost. In fall, trees and vines explode into breathtaking reds and oranges, tomatoes on the vine and perhaps an early frost. And winter, white, crisp, twinkling snow, house lights and early garden catalogues. And oh yes, a touch of frost.

Being familiar with nature's decorative change should help us move the seasons indoors and take advantage of this wondrous metamorphosis laid at our footsteps. (In winter it's called snow!) For example, during fall you won't travel very far down a road leading out of town before you hit garden stands selling this year's produce. There's corn and dill, cukes and cabbage, crabapples and apple crabs, cauliflower and much more. There's also a host of flowers, especially glads.

So what, you say?

How about a table centrepiece of local grown fruits and vegetables. You can be as fancy or plain as you wish, but what a beautiful effect. And the aroma; the bouquet given off by fresh produce is without rival!

You'll also see many grain fields and I'm sure some farmers could be persuaded to part with a small sheaf of wheat or barley for your decor. You might even offer to trade with him. Offer him your wonderful teenager as free labor for a short while.

I also like to go into the garden and cut some plants for drying, using them during the festive season. I've done the usual stuff like strawflowers, coneflowers and statice, but this year I'm trying to dry out massive heads of sedum.

If they turn out good, wonderful. If only so-so, I'll just tell everybody my wife did them!

October 16, 1994

Picture worth thousand words

I once told you that it's a good idea to bring the size of the room you are decorating to help us do a proper lay-out for you. Also, location of door openings, vents, windows, etc., are really quite useful to allow us to get a feel for the room. Another thing you might bring in is pictures — especially pictures of what you are looking for. These are really a big help to any furniture retailer.

Many people come in with pictures taken out of magazines they've bought (or magazines they've looked through at doctor's offices or hair salons — I'll never tell!).

This is really a bonus for the customer and our staff. We know what you're looking for and can hopefully find it for you.

The few anecdotes below illustrate the benefits of pictures and samples.

A while back a customer came in looking for the "California look". We showed her Southwestern, Lodge, etc., but no luck. In exasperation, she pulled out a picture of the sofa from her aunt's home in California. It was French Provincial. But because her aunt lived in California it was obviously the "California look".

Another customer came in looking for a "Teddybear" chair. We started showing her large over-stuffed chairs and recliners. As it turned out, it was a "Bergere" chair she wanted. She had simply heard the name incorrectly.

In another instance, a customer came in looking for new upholstery to match her green carpet. She was repainting her existing green walls but the carpet had to stay. Every upholstery sample we showed her did not have the right shade of green. She finally brought in a carpet sample. It was grey/beige. The reflection from her deep green walls made the carpet appear to have a greenish tint.

So bring a picture; it's worth a thousand words and (in spite of what my wife says) even I can't talk that good!

WE DO IT ALL FOR YOU

October 23, 1994

A case of "Puppy Love!"

A puppy gets away with anything! I mean anything!

Last week, my wife told me that our furniture finisher would have to pay a slight visit to our home as there was a small problem with a book table.

Small problem, hah! One whole corner was chewed off — the whole corner!

I get one teensy drop of water on a table and it's good for a 30-minute "quiet" discussion. Our new puppy uses the table as a late-night snack and it's simply a small problem.

In a more serious vein, what some people view as serious problems are usually quite easily tended to with proper staff and trade items.

Most fine furniture stores have a touch-up man on staff. He is quite different from a furniture finisher. Spot touch-ups are usually done in the home, and it's really an exceptional talent.

Refinishing usually involves sending the furniture to a refinishing shop, where the whole surface or the entire piece is stripped and refinished. This is a tough job but is usually easier to do than spot touch-ups.

Touch-ups have to be done anywhere on the piece where the damage has occurred. The repair has to be blended in so as to make is as invisible as possible.

So if there is a ring on your table because a glass resided there overnight, or if your vaccuum cleaner has "massaged" your table legs a few times too often, you don't need to buy a new table (alas!).

Simply call your friendly furniture store and have them dispatch their equally friendly touch-up man (or woman). Most dealers have very affordable hourly rates and the results are in most instances quite satisfying.

And if your husband scuffs a corner of a table, tell him he wouldn't have to sit in the corner if he'd been as cute as your puppy!

October 30, 1994

It's good to be home again!

We're back from the furniture show. We saw oodles of furniture and accessories, and picked up some terrific and some not so terrific decorating ideas.

The International Home Furnishings Show, held twice a year in North Carolina, is one of the largest of its kind in the world. It's a trend setter and attracts exhibitors and buyers from all over.

Canada has a large contingent of manufacturers displaying their wares at the show, and they do well. One of the largest is Manitoba's very own Palliser Furniture. They regularly have a large ad in Furniture Today, an excellent trade journal, and are well known in the U.S.

You get stuck on so many shuttle buses and share so many dining tables with people that the natural inclination is to strike up casual conversations. The first question we usually hear is "So where y'all from?" The next question invariably is "Where is this here Winnikreg or Winnebago?" We just tell them it's the home of Palliser Furniture and the Winnipeg Jets hockey team. Most often they say "Oh, you mean Winnipeg? Whyn'cha say so?"

There are a lot of new furniture patterns being produced, but not many new styles. Casual, in all its forms, is still a predominant style and the new collections that are presented are just newer patterns reinforcing the casual theme.

One of the most exciting patterns we viewed was a collection by Thomasville Furniture called American Revival. It was a wood series finished in a light oak that exuded warmth. Another was a country casual series by Stanley Furniture, The Norman Rockwell Collection.

The best part of the show? Coming home. I never thought I'd miss Mayor Sue threatening to cut our library and pool hours, new arena talk or my mother-in-law's pre-dawn Sunday morning calls. Keep 'em comin' Ma. Good to be home!

November 27, 1994

First snowfall is here to stay

Some called it a storm, but to a Winnipegger it was simply the 'staying' snowfall heralding in this year's festive season. There usually is a ground-coverer (my own word) or two in October and maybe a dusting in November before we get permanently mantled by that magical white cloak.

This year, however, there were no mock snowfalls and scant few dustings. This year it came last week and it ain't movin' (except on the edge of a shovel) 'till March or April.

A lot of us were caught unprepared. I mean, how can you even think of snow with that fantastic October that flowed effortlessly into November?

Snow shovels that lay buried were hastily retrieved, dusted off and put into quick service. Snow blowers, for those who would rather pitch it onto the neighbors' driveway, were also plied along our walks and driveways.

And sweaters, scarfs, earmuffs and woolens were lugged up from storage or quickly purchased and bango — winter here we come!

That takes care of the outside, for now. But how prepared were we for the inside stuff? Well, at the shop I must confess we weren't quite "Johnny at the mark!" As usual ...

The tree was still somewhere in the warehouse. The lights were not.

The ornaments had been moved and nobody remembered where.

We wanted to do something nice for the windows, but still hadn't a clue.

A silver foil tree that I was especially fond of had been discarded by the design staff.

And my wife was fit to be tied.

But we quickly moved into high gear. The boys got the tree out, found the lights and ornaments and, under the torrid tutelage of our top tree tactician, our tree was totally trimmed in traditional tidings!

We were at peace with the world (and my wife!). Terrific!

CHRISTMAS IS COMING!

December 4, 1994

Designers prove invaluable

All dressed up and ready to go? Or are you? Something doesn't feel quite right.

If you're a guy you check your tie, straighten the pleat in your trousers, brush your shoes on the back of your pants, smooth back your hair, you even look in the mirror. Everything is fine, but something is missing.

Your wife gets up, leaves the room and is back in a second. She deftly stuffs your "show" handkerchief in your jacket's breast pocket. The result — perfect!

In decorating we run into similar situations. We've helped the customer select a sofa and love seat in a style they adore and in a cover they'd thought they would never find. We've helped them with the wall and carpet coloring. The occasional tables they've selected work very well and so do the lamps ... but we ain't finished yet!

The room as it stands would be okay but you didn't come to a fine furniture store for an OK look — you could have done that yourself.

You came to get that special feeling; the drama with a touch of excitement thrown in. This is where the design staff of your furniture store is of invaluable assistance. Most fine furniture stores offer a fabulous selection of accessories to assist in this worthy endeavor.

An artificial plant on that lamp table with the light beaming down on it and a Samurai warrior in mandarin-toned rice paper can help heighten the mood and theme of an oriental setting.

A gold leaf mirror with a faux bamboo frame picks up the reflections of the framed print of Eastern cloud shrouded in subtle tones.

A few more pieces, chosen with the thoughtful care that makes the setting seem so natural and inviting. Okay? No. Perfect? You betcha.

The only trouble is, the room looks so good your wife won't let you or your buddies use it!

THE FINISHING TOUCH!

December 11, 1994

'Compatables' an exciting series

Cherry and mahogany are used in the manufacture of some of the most exquisite furniture accent pieces. The woods, rich in tone, are further enhanced by deep stains, imparting a feeling of elegance — even haughtiness — to the furniture and by association to the surroundings.

I have found that the trend today for most top manufacturers is to have a collection of accent items crafted in these two fine woods. Thomasville is no exception, and they have added to their already full line of outstanding mahogany and cherry collections some outstanding eclectic items in an exciting series entitled "Compatables". Both collections have many similar and overlapping items and some which are distinctive to that series alone. Both display tea tables. For me, elegance and practicality in crafted furniture reached a zenith not yet exceeded in the English Tea Table. This table has a height approaching that of the dining table, 30 inches or so.

You cannot sip tea, coffee, or whatever at a tea table in a slouched position. You must sit upright with proper posture, and at least pretend that our species is at least twice removed from the animal kingdom.

This is a feat unimaginable if not downright impossible for most teenagers and your wife's distant cousin, thus removing them from your eating area at family soirees.

Another serving or "munching at" table approaching respectability is the tray tea table. The leg treatment is usually ball and claw or the graceful Queen Anne "duck-bill" style.

These tables are usually somewhere in height between the stylish tea table and the average coffee tables, say near two feet high. The top lifts off and can be taken into the kitchen, loaded with goodies and returned to its stand fully stacked for the head of the house to savor.

At home, when she's through, the kids and I fight over the scraps!

TEA TIME

December 18, 1994

Make room a LIVING space

Back beyond living memory, we had a very tiny living room with a fake fireplace flanked by a sofa, love seat and an odd chair.

The sofa was against the window wall and my wife would occasionally lie down and watch the birds outside bankrupting us at our bird feeder. In the early afternoon the sun would beam down on her and she enjoyed wonderful midday naps.

When we decorated, we flanked the fireplace with two love seats and a pair of chairs facing inward. It looked fine, but without the sofa she lost her "place in the sun."

More important, when we entertained, our limited seating capacity was strained and we soon discovered two unrelated men were uncomfortable sitting together in a love seat.

Quite often room layouts are almost generically designed without taking into consideration the lifestyle of the occupants. We recently re-designed an L-shaped room in which the natural focal point at one end was to be flanked by two love seats and a pair of chairs. The other end facing the dining suite was almost barren.

We asked (this is so important!) and found out that this was a living room that had been well used. We then asked: "Does anyone ever grab a quick nap in this room?" "We both do," they chimed, and yet they had allowed their comfort to be compromised for design expediency. Don't.

The solution was to rearrange the sofa and love seat somewhat facing the focal point not flanking it. Everything suddenly opened up. We were now able to get two chairs and an exciting bench into the setting which now encompassed most of the former "barren" area as well! The room became a LIVING space, not just an extension of a floor plan.

Entertaining became easier, comfort returned, traffic areas were opened up and peace reigned in the valley once more!

January 15, 1995

Choose exciting wall treatments

"When you're new in Winnipeg all the houses are white." This was the plaintive lament of a charming young lady who came to Winnipeg from Toronto when her husband was transferred.

She marveled that with all the white around us in winter, Winnipeggers still utilized a lot of white and off-white tones in their interior color schemes. "Icy coolness" was a phrase she used.

To a degree, she's right. We have a tremendous amount of white in Winnipeg: the snow; the exterior of many of our frame houses; the ever popular Winnipeg stone (stucco); and many of our interior walls.

Why, when we have such a profusion of white in our natural surroundings, do we duplicate this monochromatic color scheme in our controllable ones? The answer seems to be that we're used to it. We're complacent with those things we're most familiar with — even white in winter!

We're often asked to recommend background colors. On the whole, we find the customer amenable to suggestions even though they may feel the tones are too strong. Because they love the layout and fabric selection, they're willing to try more exciting wall color treatments.

The paint store clerk may throw them a curve by stating that the color is too deep and he'll lighten it. They phone. We may say, "No. It'll be beautiful." Once again we're on the right track, until the painter says, "Too dark. Lemme lighten it." Second call comes in. Again we all allay the customer's fears.

The third call is the best. It can be simple or effusive. It's, "Thank you, the room looks fabulous!" It's a wonderful call!

When we redid our basement, my wife wanted a deep forest green. I wanted off-white. She agreed with me, but we got green somehow. I wouldn't tell her this but it ain't bad!

Color it Fabulous!

March 19, 1995

Discounts can be good value

So you think all large sale discounts are too good to be true? Well maybe, but ... suppose you have a discontinued China cabinet on your showroom floor. It's a beautiful piece with a price tag near $7,000. It was once part of a dining room grouping that, while beautiful, was the wrong kind of "mover". It was moved all over the showroom floor but never out the door.

Somebody bought the table and chairs only, but not the cabinet. You thought it would easily sell by itself. It was functional and attractive. It could be an equally useful piece in the living room library or wherever an attractive display cabinet would fill the bill.

That was nine months or so ago. That gorgeous piece (while still gorgeous) seems to have taken on a life of its own and with the collection now discontinued you can no longer order the table and chairs to make it a complete dining set.

Being a wise retailer, you realize you should mark down this piece with a hefty discount and clear it out, tout suite! There's a very good rationale at play here that states "Your first loss is your best loss", and it's quite true most times.

However, there's another rationale here as well. Put very simply, it avows that "If your designers think it's a wonderful piece, it ain't goin' nowhere for awhile!"

Disregarding this latter adage at great personal peril, you mark this piece down from say $7,000 to $995. It's well below cost, but if you don't clear it out quick, chances are you'll be looking at this item for some time to come.

So even though it's marked down plenty, (and even grown a moustache) it may be a wonderful value and a good piece to have around! Right?!

Too Good Too Be True?!

June 18, 1995

Picture brings back memories

There's a rather jocular picture in our family album. It could be titled, 'A day in the life of a small businessman'. It shows our family stuffing fliers early on in our existence. At this stage we had four children and our Terrier, Susie.

The oldest three kids were in their teens and my youngest daughter was still struggling through single-digit youth.

The whole family was engaged in the stuffing and stamp licking process, but my oldest son carried the system to a higher art form. He held up a stamp while the dog licked it, then placed it on the envelope!

We've even been known to let customers peer over our shoulders when we're stuffing envelopes, and then when they get close, ZAP, we press them into service and don't let them go until they've stuffed 50 or so!

As in all businesses, the process of getting out the company flyer is exciting and hectic at the same time. We usually use a covering letter whose makeup can be agonized over until every word seems perfect. The sample items chosen for this missive can be equally agonized over, especially when there is a marked difference of opinion as to which items shall be listed.

I usually handle this with some of our designers and other staff, and if we do it early enough in the morning, we can usually escape the criticism and input of a certain female principal.

However, some mornings she has been known to surface almost on time and the picnic is over. Unsolicited advice is now freely given (not offered!).

I'm sure most entrepreneurs who are part of a family business suffer likewise, but I have an ace in the hole: I can think back to that wonderful picture!

Fine Furniture Specialists!

July 2, 1995

Treat customers with respect

I went into a building supply store, stepped up to the first counter I came to and asked where the drywall bits were. There were two ladies and one, looking at me with an astonished scowl, said "over there", pointing to a distant counter.

Imagine stupid ol' me going to a counter and seeking help 'cause I didn't know where in this large building supply complex the drywall bits were located!

The chap at the bit counter was pleasant enough, especially so when compared to the reception at what I later learned was the cash counter. However, when I went to purchase a few drywall screws, a tall lummox in this department with a keen distaste for the Queen's English muttered his way belligerently through my purchase.

If it wasn't already late in the afternoon, I would have made some reference to unsuccessful evolutionary experiments and left to make my purchase elsewhere.

Truth is, there's no guarantee of better service elsewhere — and isn't that a great sadness. And now back to the women at the cash ...

Once I got there to pay for stuff and not bother them with questions, they were fine. Heck, they weren't just fine, they were downright pleasant! And yet, I betcha if I asked them why they were so feisty when I first approached the counter, they wouldn't have realized they were.

Unfortunately, this automatic response is all too common in public dealings. Many retail establishments make an effort to service clientele in a pleasant manner. The other way not only hurts the store's image, it isn't fun — for anybody!

This may sound very trite but, "it feels much nicer being nice!"

I'm even going to tell my wife about this truism (maybe when she's sleeping)!

"It feels much nicer being nice..."
zzzz

July 9, 1995

Accessorize your home

"... take your basic black dress for example ..."

This is an oft-used phrase that one of our designers uses to get across the point that accessories can really play an exciting part in decorating your 'living space'.

As with a room setting, the basic black dress can be accessorized to suit your current taste or mood. For example, a simple strand of pearls can be devastatingly beautiful by its pure simplicity.

I've also seen rooms done in this same mode. A single framed print starkly portrayed on a blank wall may say more for you than a large grouping of prints.

Carefully done, the effect of this controlled simplicity can be arrestingly beautiful (until your best friend comes over and shouts: "What happened to all the pictures?").

On the other hand, you may feel like dressing up that simple black dress in such a stunning and 'chic' fashion that your sister-in-law, in a jealous snit, won't talk to you for four weeks! (Could be worse, she could start talking again in only two weeks!)

I realize that changing accessories like wall hangings may not be as easy as changing clothes, but we're not necessarily talking about major changes in your basic furniture layout. The addition or removal of accessories can be as effective as adding or removing larger furniture items. And nowadays, with the acceptance of accessories as a major decorative accent, their availability and variety can give you many exciting new choices at little increase in cost.

At this time of year a garden metaphor may be more illustrative. I've replaced a section of annual floral plantings with a large austere rock. Both settings are correct and effective, but this year I opted for the quieter "strand of pearls" look.

And my wife thought I never paid attention to what she said!

September 24, 1995

Furniture stores come and go

I've often made reference to the fact that furniture styles come and go. Well, believe it or not, the same thing happens to furniture stores!

A young lady was in our showroom one day when a bit of nostalgic thought was floating through my mind and I asked her: "Do you remember Genser's?"

Earlier, on the way to work, I had asked my youngest heir the same question and received a blank stare in return. So I was really pleased that not only did she remember that former Winnipeg furniture store, she also remembered the location, "down on Portage right by the Capitol theatre."

So I got my young scion to go the library for me, where they keep some terrific records on the third floor. The staff is really helpful and he was able to get photostats of the 'Retail Furniture' section from some old phone books.

He brought back a photostat from the 1949 book and the listing that really shook me up was a store on north Main Street called Lord's Furniture. I had completely forgotten about it, and yet when it opened its doors there was quite a lot of hoopla. I was just a wee tyke then, but my wife tells me the "Press" reported that their showroom windows were the tallest in Western Canada! And they had a record department where you could listen to your favorite music. Talk about progress!

Other names from the past that appeared in the phone book and that I had some familiarity with were Globe Radio and Furniture, Empire Radio, McKeag Furniture, Nefco Furniture, and of course Wilson's.

One of the best (?) ads was a display ad that read: "For Furniture Phone - - - - - - (6 numbers!), Easy Terms, Trades Accepted".

That's all there was, no other information, no name, no address.

You could ask, Where are they now? But heck, you didn't even know where they were then!

Winnipeg's Trusted Dining Centre

October 29, 1995

No room at the inn

We've just come back from the "big" semi-annual furniture show in North Carolina and I know I should talk about what I've seen and how exciting or otherwise it was, but I'm just bursting with other "news?"

You see, this October I went down not only with my dear wife but we took two of our children who are actively involved in "Brick's" (one willingly, the other when we can catch him) with us. We booked two separate rooms. We arrivèd at the hotel and only one room was available.

Four of us had to share one hotel room, with two beds, thank goodness! But — and this is a big one — only one bathroom!

I'm not saying that I didn't get my fair share of bathroom time. I was allotted the same amount of time as the female members of our party and the other male who accompanied us (and can whine in an uncanny and frightening manner that not only reaches his mother's heartstrings but can play a jig on them!).

As I say, I did receive the same hour and a half the others demanded, but I don't think between 2-3:30 a.m. is a particularly good time for brushing one's teeth.

The next morning we frantically had our office fax our reservation to the hotel.

One room was reserved under Fred Brick, the other under Lisa Stuart — instead of Lisa and Stuart Brick.

While I, at 11 in the evening, was desperately trying to reach the housing group that reserves most of the rooms at showtime, the desk clerk was amusing my wife by reading to her the names of people with reserved rooms who hadn't shown yet.

He did read off the name Stuart, but it didn't click with my wife. I'm not saying that I would have cottoned to it right away but sometimes, when you're a drop older things can slip by you. Eh Dear?

Room for Everybody!

December 10, 1995

Memories are of This...

I've just read about a chap who claims that furniture gets a bum rap! He says it's looked upon as "grandfatherly" stuff, you know, items for us old guys and gals which lack the excitement of the current fads like computers, Cars, R.V.'s or snappy clothes. Also, there's probably a whole bunch of other distractions competing for our `discretionary' (Hah!) dollars.

And while cars and computers and some of the other good stuff are darn near essential in today's hectic world there's nothing that compares with the warmth and lasting family relationships built around certain furniture items in the home . . .

Driving somewhere with your family in the car can be pleasant enough (as long as the kids have gone to the bathroom beforehand!) but it can't compare to the warmth engendered around a supper or dining table. Even the card table in our house has been the place where memories of some `wild' cribbage and `Sergeant-major' games have been played (fought would be a more apt description!).

The jigsaw puzzle on the rec' room table (or floor!) with my wife screaming· "Don't start that thing, you'll make a big mess down here!". Then at 3:00 A.M., when all sensible people have retired for the night, guess whose wife is squinting under the harsh light working on the puzzle?

And who isn't warmed by the sight of the family sofa, the one the dog is finally allowed to lie on but two of your kids are not!

And if you want a little harsh reality, your dining suite isn't going to be outdated like your computer, - before you get it home!

And it'll probably be worth more a year from now while your new car takes an "auto"-matic 20% or 30% "bath" each and every year!

Furniture in reality is very much like furniture store owners. Their beauty and value increase with the passage of time. Even my wife knows this!

Your Home Comfort Centre!

January 28, 1996

The Guessing Game

We're always reading about predictions and forecasts. It can be a thankless job, for instance the Weatherman gets abuse when he's wrong and little or no reward if he's right.

Well, furniture manufacturers do the same thing. They have designers that predict, after a fashion, (excuse the pun) what they think the consumer will like and more importantly, buy!

This is actually a process that involves three major commitments.

Firstly the manufacturer has to construct the showroom models to show to prospective buyers at furniture shows or at private viewings.

Secondly, the retailer must make a commitment. If he likes the new offering, he's got to put his money where his mouth is by buying the group. If he's really sold on it he might even buy it in depth, that is, he may commit to increasing his orders of the articles he bought so that if and when (and hopefully when) the series "takes off" he'll have back-up stock and won't run out immediately!

The third commitment is a very important one. It's what makes the other two turn, survive, go forward, persist, persevere, etc. - get the idea? It's the ultimate purchase of the goods by the consumer. If the customer ain't buying the previous two ain't eatin' too well!

Shaker furniture styles were an example of a trend that hit high approval ratings on the manufacturers display floor, the retailers showroom and best of all in the consumer's home.

We carried a Shaker series by Thomasville called "Solitaire" and it was an outstanding success. One of the best in the business was by the Canadian maker, Shermag.

And any retailer 'worth his salt' or better still who wanted to do more than just 'stay' in business devoted a fair amount of space to a Shaker Collection.

Marriage is the same way. You're predicting what life will be like with your partner. My wife sure got lucky!

I THINK WE'VE GOT A WINNER

February 4, 1996

Oh, The Weather Outside is Frightful....

I was reading in a trade journal about the havoc wrought in the retail industry by the spate of storms that rocked the East in January.

Some of these storms occasioned the closing of stores for at least a day or two and at times longer. It wasn't the cold so much although that was bad enough, it was that fluffy white stuff.

These cities, not used to receiving large snowfalls aren't equipped to handle it and can remain clogged while a valiant but insufficient number of machines tries to restore some semblance of order.

Stores in these climes lose a number of 'sale days' that are almost impossible to recover. January is the traditional sale month for furniture. Many stores book advertising well in advance and can't stop it once it's been scheduled.

Newspaper, T.V. and radio can be ringing out your 'message' while your clientele is stuck at home in snow-clogged driveways! And the last thing on their minds is a furniture sale!

In Winnipeg we've kinda had a similar problem. While the snowfall in January was nothing much the cold sure was! (And is!) Traffic was down in retail stores for part of January while our temperatures remained similar to those enjoyed by Penguins!

But Winnipegers can't stay cloistered for too long. Thirty, forty below it don't matter, by the time the weekend hits we've got to get out of the house and shopping is a natural uplifter!

The past two weekends we've been run off our feet and I hear the same thing happened in most shopping centers!

To top it off, when my wife, an international expert on the cold chill, heard that we were just days away from breaking a cold snap record. She decided we should "go for it!" and most of us "nuts" here agree! Crazy? Nah. Just Winnipeggers!

February 25, 1996

If It Ain't Broke ...

How many times have you changed (or recovered) your sofa?

What about your living room occasional tables and legs? And that family room furniture, even if you haven't changed it yet there's a good chance you're thinking about it!

And the list can go on and on like the kitchen suite or those bookcases that seemed so suitable a while back and that now you'd like to give to your brother-in-law, no questions asked!

But it confounds me no end that this list stops dead short of the bedroom. As a matter of fact chances are that your bedroom suite is almost the only item of furniture in the home that you haven't changed. And it's not because it's such an exquisite collection of pieces. In fact, if the truth be told it's probably kind of ordinary and yet quite serviceable - and therein may lie the answer!

It's not so showy that you can easily become tired of it and its very practicality may be the secret to its longevity.

I know several people of my vintage who have Teak bedroom suites. (Never mind how I know Cynthia, I just know!)

The styling is quite basic and utilitarian and the wood (like most husbands) still looks good and holds up well.

This very practicality is probably the main reason for not replacing it. In other words, 'If it ain't broke, don't fix it!'

And the other prime reason? Well it don't take much guessing. I think it's because there always seems to be something the house or family needs that's more important than a new bedroom suite. Besides it's where the kids crawled up on with their sore throats or bruised egos.

It's where the dog sleeps during the day when you're not home. (I know these things!)

Besides, how could you possibly get rid of something that you've shared half your life with and still looks that good?

Right dear?

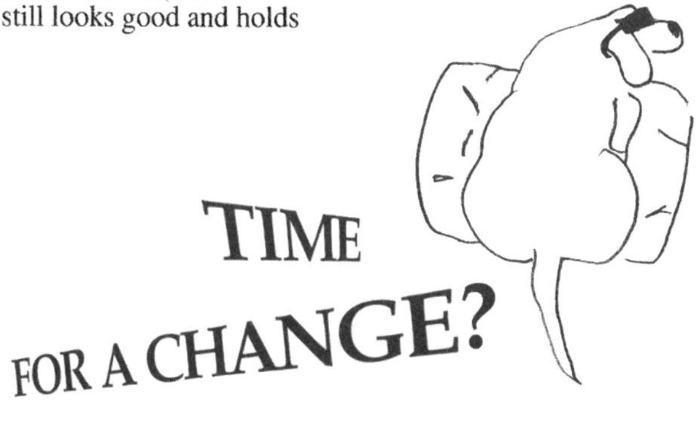

March 10, 1996

The Winter of Our Discontent

It's the beginning of March and it's Breakout Time! Those of you lucky enough to 'spring' for a holiday this past season got some relief from our 'Worst Winter this Century'. Those of us who had to stay behind and turn out the lights are not bitter at all!

But many I spoke to said that when they returned and experienced the severe biting and gripping cold that found a permanent home in our "turf", the ecstasy of the holiday quickly disappeared. Reality hit them like a ton of Brick's! (No Relative! As I said I'm not bitter!).

Some people on the other hand know how to 'really' break the Winter Woes. Cast forth the Cabin Fever and say Baloney to the Blahs. They spend their money on more permanent things that give rise to wondrous good feelings.

They buy furniture!

And if there is a season for certain types of furniture, this is the season for bedroom suites. While the flock of early summer weddings is a factor it's also the time for those brave souls who have 'weathered' the winter together to celebrate the "Rite of Passage" to a warmer season.

What more fitting area to 'reward' than the dormitory which protected us from one-third of Jack Frost's gusty Gales!

This is also the time when any furniture store worth its salt will be promoting bedroom suites and the selection around town should be terrific!

I might add that the "bedroom wall" type of suite where the headboard is part of an entire wall with mirrors, lights and tons of storage is quickly becoming scarce and if you haven't seen these, take a gander, they're wonderful not to mention practical and exciting at the same time!

My wife thought we needed a new bedroom suite this year but I told her. "No Way!" Now for some reason there's a chill in our bedroom. I think she left the window open.

March 10, 1996

Big Bad Biker Mama!

We have unleashed a monster upon the Earth! Well, sort of .... Let me back up a bit and tell you of our travail.

Bright and early a few weeks ago my dear wife and I arrived at the office. We now have a "deli" called IRA'S in our lower quarters and on the pretense of "checking the boiler" my wife descended into the depths to grab a coffee and probably a minute (hah!) morsel of Ira's famous chocolate cheesecake.

Near the bottom her descent quickened. She fell and broke her foot in two places. It was awful!

At the hospital she was 'casted' and told to stay home and stay still. Those of you who know Cynthia also know that keeping her home is next to impossible and keeping her still is an effort in futility.

We were at work the next day and she accompanied me to Chicago a few days later! The break got worse and she was ordered to keep all weight off the broken foot! Period!

She got a pair of crutches and a wheelchair and all was almost peaceful again until, on one of our trips to the excellent doctors at Health Sciences she spotted a motorized scooter.

End of peace!

She asked for (demanded is more like it!) a scooter. I sensed foreboding but she blinked her eyes and looked down demurely. I ordered one.

Overnight, nah not that long, instantly!, a stranger was in our midst! Where once stood a refined, mature woman of stature was now, sitting astride this machine, a motorized old broad scooting around the showroom with something approaching reckless abandon.

The staff are terrified!

She's become "Hell on Wheels!" Nothing is sacred! Not a toe nor an ankle. Even a shin is not safe from Manitoba's Mechanized Mama! And she wants a leather jacket! With frills yet!

The scratch and dent sale begins soon!

We Got It All ...

Bedrooms -
Dining Rooms -
Sofas - and
The Biker Mama!

March 31, 1996

THE JOY (& HORROR) OF HABERDASHERY

When I go shopping for clothes it's really as an addendum to my wife's looking for a blouse or something. The last time I got waylaid into helping her find ONLY a blouse she found three of them! She also found two skirts and a "very necessary" business suit. (Does this mean the other five business suits weren't necessary?)

By the time it came my turn to look for a shirt I was so enveloped in terror that we had to leave!

The women in my family (wife and two daughters) think that without at least two of them present I dare not go shopping.

So, it came as a bit of a shock when, this past Wednesday, I showed up at the office with two pairs of pants, a vest, a jacket and a shirt. While I was thus engaged in spreading around larder in men's wear, I was able to observe first-hand, without instruction from the softer (HAH!) side of our family, the current offerings in clothing.

Even though I have stated that the 'casual look' is big in furniture and relaxed is the "in" thing and even though I've often pointed out how closely furniture parallels fashion modes, I was absolutely shocked at the variety and choice available in 'casual' and 'relaxed' styling!

Most choices I found were quite pleasant, especially sport shirts with a soft hand or feel. In fact some were downright "snuggly"! (I bought one of these and if it 'works' at home I'll buy shares in the company!)

Yet, with all the hullabaloo about casual, relaxed and softness etc., guess what? - some formal styles, stuff we ain't seen for a few years are starting what could become a major revival.

You know Cynthia, it just goes to show you, the older, or rather more mature and good - looking styles in furniture never stay out of fashion for very long! Sorta reminds you of furniture dealers. Right? Funny, I don't hear you!

May 26, 1996

Put Your Money Where Your House Is!

There's a clientele out there that would dearly love to purchase quality furniture but we're making it difficult for them to find. I think its roots are fear based. Fear that today's people have been through too many recessions and economic cycles and will not readily spend more money on consumer goods than is absolutely necessary.

This idea cannot help but be reinforced if you listen to furniture ads on the radio, watch them on T.V., or read them in the papers and those endless flyers. The message that comes across loud - really loud - and clear in most of the industry's retail advertising is that cheaper is better.

Well, it ain't so!

Less expensive may be a way to go for those just starting out or for those whose priorities are not that focused on finer furniture. Heck, we don't all drive Cadillacs or Mercedes but we sure know where to find them if we want them!

And maybe that explains some of the problem. If we want to sell goods that are in the upper end of the income scale, maybe we should be telling more people that we have them.

Another problem may be that furniture, unlike cars or other big ticket items like jewellery, are not displayed on the outside but in the confines of our homes and we'd rather put our money into items that give us "exterior status".

And if I may take this a step further, it seems that exterior status is a male thing and us guys just don't recognize the worth of quality items that can't be displayed to the outside world.

I know that this really isn't the case, so I discussed it with my wife. She snickered. So I went to a higher court, I asked my daughters. Alas, their minds had been poisoned by their mother. I feel so bad I think I'll go buy a new car - you know, one of those flashy ones with fins and glittery paint and ...

Beautiful Furniture,
Beautifully Made...

June 2, 1996

We've Got The Right Model!

A chap I knew held a swimsuit event - in the middle of Winter! He sold motorcycles and in Winnipeg these ain't big movers in January! So, in an effort to spruce up sales a bit, especially on bike accessories he offered a deal to the first few ladies who surfaced in swimsuits, especially Bikinis.

And the people came! In Winnipeg, a Bikini in January is worth leaving home for!

I was reminded of this while reading about Calvin Klein and Antonio.

Who, you might say, is Antonio? Apparently he's a marvellous new `Hunk' who wears and promotes others to wear men's undies by Calvin Klein.

One day recently, Macy's Herald Square store ran a full page ad featuring the gorgeous Antonio in the briefest of briefs and a few lines of copy. That's all!! The copy stated that Antonio would be at the Macy's locale between 12:00 and 2:00 that day and would autograph any Calvin Klein undie purchase. It was a dismal day but a thousand people made the trek and 400 bought a pair of step-ins! That's a 40% effective promo! It don't get much better!

And not only did they buy at the starting price of $14.00 a pair, but most sales were in the higher or stratosphere bracket! And when you get a thousand people wandering through your store they're sure to make a few other purchases.

So I told my wife that if we had some sexy hunk perched on a sofa with tight, almost painted on jeans and a "T" shirt over his shoulder, barely hiding the muscles on his bare chest, maybe we would sell a lot more sofas or something.

"You gonna get Antonio?" she asked.

I said, (In jest of course!), "Maybe I'll model."

A smirk would have sufficed Cynthia, 'cause I certainly didn't appreciate the throaty horse laughs. But the pounding on the coffee table and rolling on the floor, doubled over yet, was really excessive!

BEST
DRESSED
SOFAS
IN TOWN!

June 9, 1996

Finish With A Flair (Or A Tiger!)

How many times have you heard the expression,'If you ain't got a giraffe at home, you ain't got nothin''? And of course the addendum,'If you ain't got a zebra to keep it company, you really ain't livin'!

"Good gracious Holmes!," you might say, "he's gone mad!"

But I haven't, 'cause I'm not talking real live animals, I'm talkin' those big animal statues with the wonderful glazes on them that look so real! I'm talkin' about accessory items that set a mood whether excitement or contentment or somewhere in between!

Now don't get me wrong, furniture is wonderful and exciting plus a few other adjectives but accessories, well that's a whole new ball game.

How else can you pet a 'wild' tiger and not get bitten? Or approach a 'shiny' (brass) gazelle and not scare him away?

You can savour the flavour of pomegranates in a wicker basket that always stay fresh and admire the gorgeous profusion of tropical plants that are always lush. Simply Dee-lush-us!

We even have a very colourful cat that can outstare you or your most menacing elementary school teacher and then gaze out the window for hours and hours, never howling to go outside!

We have a single, large, pure white rose, breathtakingly beautiful and hauntingly chaste, that hasn't dropped a petal or leaf in months, if ever!

And if you gaze upon our walls you'll find a Da Vinci lady with piercing eyes and a severe, unsmiling mouth. But look further and you'll find a sultry siren in a fur-trimmed satin gown, lounging on a chaise, with a very inviting smile on her lips and eyes that seem to speak volumes!

(She's only a friend Cynthia, really!)

We have fish for bookends and a Cheetah for your bed! We got crystal balls and metal horses, ships on the wall and elephants on a chest.

Incidentally, I almost bought a wild looking Tiger statue but I already work with a live one!

(Just kidding dear. Honest!)

June 23, 1996

Take This Job and - Take It Home!

There are really 2 types of home office. One is an actual room in the house designated as such, replete with all the necessary accounterments (I know it's a big word Cindy!). There's a stationery desk with computer acceptance capacity, book shelves, filing cabinets and all the other good stuff for making the recently vacated (sometimes not willingly) bedroom into the home office.

The other home office is not confined to a specific room in the house. It bears a striking resemblance to an armoire which is actually a big door chest that costs more when you call it by a French name. It can resemble an entertainment centre too, also a big chest that costs more when you call it something else.

These "home offices" do well as furniture almost anywhere in the house, but when you open the doors, voila! There's a desk with a glaring monitor and bookshelves and pigeon holes above. Below a pull-out tray holds your keyboard. This "armoire"/"entertainment centre" will hold all the other computer paraphernalia such as printer, tower, CD Rom modem and incidentals like files, paper, staples, whiteout (not for the screen, honey) and a picture of Roxy your dog.

Some also have what looks like an iron board fastened on the right side (left side for southpaws) which, when brought down becomes a run-off desk that addresses the need for work area elbow room. It can also hold your kids' crayon pictures and a photo of that once-was girlfriend - that you married!

Concealability and compactness are the keys to these new-age offices which have not just appeared, but exploded onto the furniture scene. And most of us furniture guys display and catalogue a goodly number of them.

My wife, who always thinks of me, says we should take one home so I can finally do some work. But why did she snicker?

BRINGIN' HOME
THE BACON!!
&
THE BUSINESS!
Sizzle

July 7, 1996

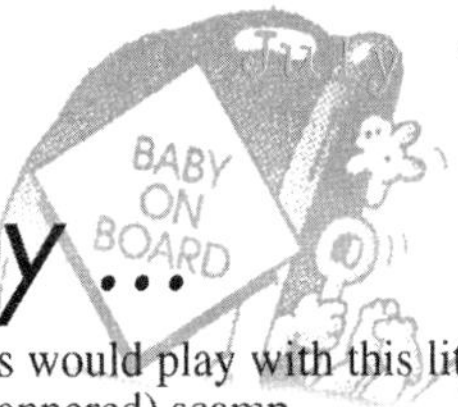

Rock-A-Bye Baby . . .

We are in the doldrums of summer. I'm usually not this dead tired 'til August but the heat, combined with the fact that my wife has worked me savagely these past seven days, has left me with little time to mull on the meandering of the Furniture Trade. Instead I'll relate a few light hearted anecdotes that we've experienced.

We started out in a suite in a 2nd floor warehouse with 3 children (not for sale!). At the time and while we were there we had another daughter whom we raised "in the business"!

We would bring her carriage to work and use it as a crib/stroller (unbeknownst to Child and Family Services!) and she soon learned to sleep through anything.

One day a woman shopping in the store approached the carriage, which my wife had briefly positioned close to the freight elevator, a noisy cantankerous behemoth, the elevator that is. The poor lady thought the object in the carriage was a lifelike doll. She couldn't resist. She leaned over and touched the doll. It moved, the lady shrieked, my wife bolted out of the office and caught the lady before she fell!

As an aside, we eventually got a playpen in the office and staff and customers would play with this little, (well-mannered) scamp.

Well, 16 years or so later we had a very talented lady finisher who brought her baby to work when she serviced merchandise in our shop. We bought a playpen/crib for the office and staff and customers once again looked after a baby while Mommy worked.

Well it seems that time, at times, does stand still. An old customer of ours walked in one day, took a look at the playpen laden with child and, as if it were only yesterday - said "You've still got that baby here?!"

My wife in one of her few attempts at humour, looked at the baby, then at me and said: "Which one?!"

September 8, 1996

THOUGHTS, AT THE AIRPORT

I just dropped my daughter and sister off at the airport. They're going to my brother's son's wedding in Toronto. Why didn't I just say nephew? - and of course, my soon-to-be new niece. I'm going tomorrow with more of the gang.

But back to the airport, as we approached the gate area a distinguished looking gentleman with white hair (all us guys with white hair look very distinguished, it drives our wives crazy!) remarked: "There's that furniture man!" And then he added: "I recognize you from your picture!" I held up my hand and with thumb and forefinger made a small box and said: "From the little snapshot?" "Yep" he said (Us distinguished guys can get away with words like yep and you bet!!!!! - and that really drives our wives crazy!)

At the beginning when I first started doing this column we always thought that demographically we would attract an older, more mature audience, you know like us white haired guys but comments have come from all walks of life and the experience is very humbling.

Besides all this stuff there's one big problem, topics! My wife (who else) is always criticizing the way I stray away from furniture subjects to other topics, like this article for instance. But it really isn't planned this way.

This week I had intended to do a piece on the new Fall colours and patterns. Stuff like the gorgeous new earth tone florals and the exciting new paisleys not to mention the exotic tapestry introductions. I had intended to read a tremendous new article in our trade magazine on this very subject and I would be just bursting with vital information.

But the gentleman at the airport touched a responsive chord and goodbye Fall colors till maybe next week and hello Cynthia with: "What's with this airport business? What's the airport got to do with furniture? And why are you talking to strange guys at airports?" But I daren't give back any sassy answers 'cause my birthday's next week.

October 13, 1996

CONSUMER CHASE

This coming week I'll be leaving to attend a "really big shew". It's the annual International Home Furnishings Market held at High Point North Carolina. We'll be treated to a viewing of lots of new product that's been specially developed for this market with hopes from manufacturers that some of the offerings will "click" giving them a "winner". Traditionally, what drove the development of new product in this industry were things like Intuition, what your sales force says is a 'comer', what your competitors are doing and anecdotal testimony.

Having a top designer that could "flesh" out these assumptions of course goes without saying - but I'm still saying it!

This approach, while based on some excellent insight and experience has lately been looked at as akin to throwing 'ideas' at the wall and seeing which one would stick (read sell!). A lot of time and money was spent in introducing new product at each market with, as I say, hopes that one or two series would be successful.

The costs of producing literature and building inventory for groups that didn't make it only added to the cost of those that did.

A group of manufacturers, wanting to eliminate some of the guesswork and expense out of new product introductions adopted a different posture. They began conducting consumer research in order to determine what the customer wanted.

What an absolutely novel idea! Ask the end user, the consumer, what he or she wants, then try to build it for him at a reasonable price!

I thought the idea was so good that I tried it out at home. I talked with my wife and straightened her out on some of the things I would like to see happening at home. She listened, nodded, then called up her Mother who must have told her a joke 'cause they both howled a lot! She didn't tell me that joke but grins a lot when she sees me.

DESIGNING WAYS

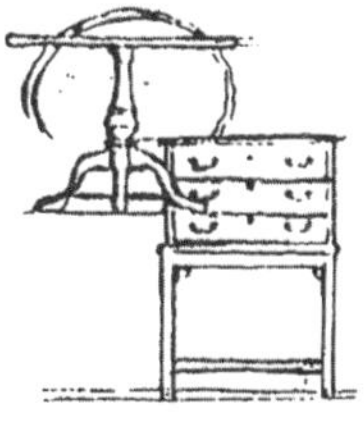

October 20, 1996

SLEEPING BEAUTIES

A while back, I wrote about the new look occurring in the bedroom. The theme was: Big is beautiful and it was emphasized most by the dramatic look and size of the bed itself.

Well, the look, not only did not dissipate, it got better: - and bigger, bolder, brasher, boisterous and even beautiful.

For the past few days at the furniture show, I've been treated to a preview of bedroom largeness, especially as regards the bed itself.

The sleigh bed, the sleek beauty that transported many to the land of nod has taken on dimension. In some its curves are highly exaggerated, and seems almost "fluid".

In others, Its additional "weight" makes it a huge piece of lumber with a curve or roll on the top rail giving it only a nodding acquaintance with its namesake and yet, if done well it can be very dramatic.

Poster beds are not only "in" but the size and height of these beauties emphasize that size is very important in the bedroom Some of these posts seem to soar upward, beautifully carved and tapering with a final cap.

For instance the rice poster bed, a longtime favorite, is no longer an understated beauty, it's now big and bold. The carving is larger and the long fluting gives it an uplifting mood.

Other posts not only look big, they also have drama because of their size. Most of these posts are "worked". That is, they have some detailing, whether it be fluting, twists or patterned assemblies which becomes a secondary attraction to their bigness.

Because the beds are so large, night tables need to be a good size just to be in scale - and they are! In fact most so called night tables are fair sized 3 or 4 door chests and quite handsome on their own. A lot have stone or polished marble tops which add to their "weight" and beauty.

I told my wife we could accommodate some larger sizes in our bedroom. She said Amen.

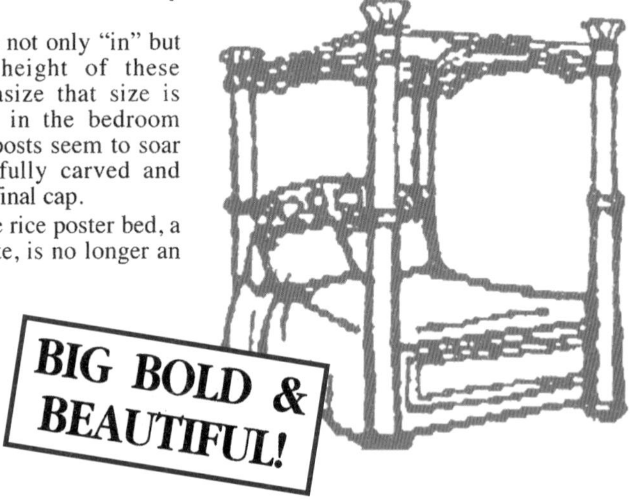

November 24, 1996

WE GOT A NICHE!

How would you like to wander into a 100,000 square foot furniture store brimming with furniture, accessories, wall hangings and all the other good things that make it a furniture store?

Fun? For some maybe, but for most of us, I don't think so!

We're now in the age of the superstore and while certain categories of merchandise are okay in this type of setting, furniture "ain't one of 'em!". After awhile, I would think even looking for anything in a space that would normally house a small arena can become quite tedious and very imposing.

In fact, I think walking into a "barn" that large containing articles of furniture, some of which are large in themselves, would be very intimidating. These are items of magnitude and you begin to wonder just how much mass can one shopper digest?

It's hard enough to absorb quantities of stuff like towels, linens, and kid's clothing which are bought on a regular basis, but trying to get a handle on the sheer variety, colour and size of furniture items available in a setting this huge, is nothing is not downright intimidating!

Some of these superstores are now experiencing a backlash with consumers going back to their "local" stores. I read in our trade journal that: "... manufacturers were talking about the little guys ... the niche players (that's us Cindy!). They're saying that we're the ones with personality and an attachment to our customers.

This describes a lot of stores in any trading area, from large to small. The stores that realize they "can't dance at every wedding" nor want to! They found their niche, whether it be high, low or medium priced furniture. Stores where the customers is comfortable and shopping is an enjoyable experience, not a daunting one!

So I told my wife: "We've got a niche." She mutters something about: "So scratch it!" She just don't understand big business.

We've Got What You're Looking For!

December 1, 1996

DIALOGUE WITH DAD

Frogs don't read much but some are terrific at holding up books!
And a couple of 'scaly', large mouthed bass can do the same thing while standing on their heads!
No dear I haven't lost my mind, I've just been "walking the Walk" in our showroom and seeing what's available in home office accessories. The frogs and fish are actually brass bookends and like most fine furniture stores we have a terrific display of den, library, office or home office accessories at this time of year.
I really enjoy the varied assortment of bookends that are available but I have a daughter that natters (yes Lisa, natters!) at me to mention other things for dens and offices. Like a magnifying glass on a brass stand. But I say: "Why not talk about those two blubbery, brass, walrus bookends that can support any weighty tome?"
But she insists I mention the exquisite black marble spheres on brass stands. But I'd rather talk about the two bookends displaying a pair of indolent cats perched on a burl-like lacquered block and peeking over the sides.
She says I should talk about the burgundy, almost opalescent sphere perched on a stark, contemporary, wrought iron base. But I say: "What about the Old World sphere and the celestial sphere that are paired as bookends?"
"But what about the large hourglass timer, or the quaint inkwell stands or the old world mini-globe on a stand?" she asks.
"But I'd have to leave out the gorgeous Greek horse bookends not to mention the pair of large agate stone bookends on acrylic bases, their rough exterior side belying the gorgeous polished face of their display surface ..." I tell her.
Finally, looking exasperated she says what sounded like: "Dad, you're driving me crazy!"
"What?!" I ask.
She says: "My mind's getting hazy."
So I told her to rest for awhile. Like her sister Marsha, she's a wonderful cook and loves animals but I think she better leave merchandising to a pro!

BOOKENDS & OTHER GOOD STUFF

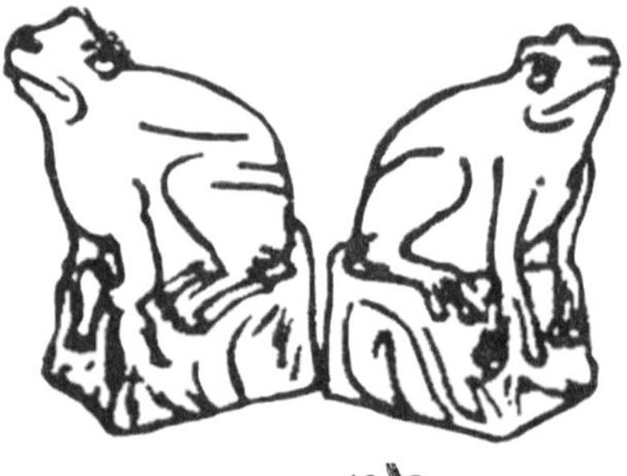

Merry Christmas to all! December 22, 1996

OUR STAFF, A CUT ABOVE!

Business cycles, birthdays and stuff come and go but for me Christmas has always been a watershed time of year. A time to stop, reflect and hopefully not repeat the past year's mistakes. Thank those who blessed your life and forgive them that didn't.

I really dislike those business columns that thank all their nebulous staff and tell you how wonderful they are, but I'm going to do it anyway 'cause without 'em we wouldn't have had this fabulous last year!

Our two shippers Ray and Mike and their neophyte helper Stuart do everything from boiler maintenance, to drywalling, to chasing pigeons out of our fifth floor, but the team really shines when it comes to crating. About 40% of our sales are out of Winnipeg and we ship from anywhere in Canada, to places as far away as Saudi Arabia, with confidence!

This wouldn't have happened if Les Girls, my wife, and Linda and Gail, our design crew, hadn't formulated such wonderful layouts and fabulous furniture and accessory placements!

When not immersed in design they're helping customers and being ably assisted by our competent sales staff. Dorothy, who came to purchase something years ago and never went home. Lisa, my youngest daughter, who like her sister, graces my life and Anne, our newest saleslady who takes a back seat to nobody!

And there's Andy, our resident touch-up man. He's so good (just ask him!) he goes by the moniker of "The Magic Man"!

And where would we be without our tireless front desk anchor man David who amazingly keeps his cool and ties it all together!

"You mention about the staff and everyone agrees they're a "crack team" but what about the customers?"

"I'm going to dear."

"Sure, like everything else, you'll forget ... I almost finished this whole article and there's nothing about our terrific customers. They deserve a special thank you. Why don't you say something about that?"

"I don't have to dear."

"And why not?"

"'cause you just did!"

Merry Christmas to all!

Linda Marchand

Dorothy Zawatsky

FRED & CYNTHIA

January 19, 1997

YOU CAN GO HOME AGAIN!

Last weekend we attended the Canadian Furniture Show in Toronto. We've attended this event but briefly in the past five to ten years but this year we were there for three full days and who says you can't go home again?! I saw so many old friends and colleagues that my cup almost runneth over! And talk about exciting product, my son said: "You know Dad the American shows are way bigger (that's the way kids talk) but this Canadian one has got more different stuff."

Translation: At the American shows you view a certain dominant style pattern or colour preference and no matter which manufacturer you attend you're almost sure to see variations of these same styles or colours tediously repeated.

However at the Canadian show most booths seemed to display different and unique collections.

There were large (even HUGE!) Armoire chests from such diverse areas as Indonesia and Mexico done in a rustic, almost crude fashion.

We saw carvings of animals that you just had to take home, like cats, perched on and peering over a shelf. dogs in chairs watching TV and holding a remote, and more cats. Tall giraffes and stodgy elephants and more cats till my daughter stepped in and said: "No more cats Dad, O.K.?"

Found another great picture line and a tapestry collection that is breathtaking and a fabulous area carpet line that I've searched for in vain (that's not a city Cynthia) at US markets.

And office furniture for the "Home" office or the "Office" office. Did we ever find great office furniture! We did business with this firm years ago and it's nice to come home again especially with their new manager, an old friends of ours. Gerry Cockerill.

And there's still more, but that's another story ... And get this, my kid (some kid he's eighteen feet tall!) makes another astute comment, he says, "There's no leisure entertainment nearby". Translation: "Dad, there's no Hooter's bar near our hotel" Just kidding dear!

February 16, 1997

LIFE WITHOUT LINT OR GITB*

The flannel nightie is out, finished, kaput!!! A franchised network of interior designers has issued its top 10 predictions for the coming year and one of them states unequivocally, positively and in a most decisive manner that one of the top ten trends in home fashions for 1997 will be, (are you listening dear?): "Glamour In The Bedroom!"

Now far be it for me to state that women of my ken, or any woman for that matter, are not fair in flannel or that they even own such a fuzzy garment. I just state the rules for the coming year so that certain people will not be caught floundering in fleece. After all: "Glamour In The Bedroom" denotes a luxuriousness that has a certain flimsy whimsy attached to it. (C'est bon!)

One of the other predictions I have a need to address is called "Relaxed Luxury". Some of the key elements of this trend are that, "... fabrics will lose their sheen for a washed or softer look." And also, "... Luxury is not stiff or opulent but inviting ..." This trend has been pooh poohed for so long, in so many different venues and under so many different names - from "Shabby Chic" to "Dressed down Fridays" to "Casual Elegance" - that I can't help falling asleep whenever I read about it!

Another forecast giving me a smidgen of grief is entitled, "Upholstery Collage". This is the practice of adorning upholstery items with more than one cover producing a patchwork effect. I have finally started to accept a very limited percentage of these offerings but I still find many to be somewhat beyond my taste. Way, way beyond!

And I'd like to share a delightful fax I received re the article on "service" last week:

REMEMBER ...

DELIVERING HIGH QUALITY SERVICE TO CLIENTS IS LIKE MAKING LOVE TO A GORILLA.

YOU DON'T STOP WHEN YOU'RE SATISFIED. YOU STOP WHEN THE GORILLA IS SATISFIED.

Now excuse me for a few hours while I explain this to my wife. Grrr ...

Bedroom Glamour?!

February 23, 1997

WHAT'S IN A NAME?

Now besides designer and celebrity named furniture other persons associated with the furniture business are predicting that in the world of colour 1997 will be "... the year of paprika" and will feature a "warm, earthy, more yellow palette (which) also includes rich amber, cinnabar and tobacco against a backdrop of moss green or yellow-green". Accent colour will be provided by "... fields of purple heather". I'm actually a fan of these tones and I'll be looking forward to viewing the fall offerings.

Another fashion trend supposed to be in the offing for this year will be tiger stripes and leopard spots. In other words the big cats are back! And they'll be shown in " ... many fashion conscious products ... (such as) ... duvet covers area rugs (and) wall coverings" ... not to mention some pretty exciting upholstery applications. Statues of these gorgeous beasts are also a highlight and are an exciting showroom feature.

I think I'll sleep on a Julia Roberts tonight and sit around with a Kim Bassinger tomorrow!

Sound far-fetched? Not really if you take one of the up and coming furniture trends into consideration. The furniture industry is not just moving into endorsements of their products by celebrities, they're moving into "Branding" entire collections with the names of noted people especially top designers like Ralph Lauren and Alexander Julian.

Other noted personalities like athletes and stars will also get into the picture. Some collections are already being touted by names like Arnold Palmer and Bob Timberlake.

So relax all you people out there, when I'm yapping about sleeping on a Julia Roberts I'm of course referring to a mattress set that may one day be part of a collection featuring her name.

Same as if you're sitting on a Ralph Lauren, chair that is, or looking for your shirt in an Alexander Julian, armoire chest of course. But back to speaking of celebrity collections and endorsements, my wife always said she'd like Paul Newman's shoes under her bed. I've never heard of that brand before and I never knew his last name ended in "s"!

Put a Tiger
in Your
Tank
House!

March 16, 1997

A BEDTIME STORY ... SORT OF!

Now I know St. Patrick's day is tomorrow and some of you might think this is just a lot of "Blarney" but I heard that RTA mattresses were a hit at a recent housewares show. This was really hard to believe. You see RTA stands for Ready-To-Assemble and it refers to furniture that you buy in pieces and put together at home. Whoever heard of RTA mattresses!!

But this past January, at The International Housewares Show in Chicago a specialty sleep division of a national company brought bedding! And it was a real show stopper!

The housewares show normally features all kinds of home products and the giants of this industry like Rubbermaid, General Electric and Sunbeam are usually sporting several dozen new products, with celebrities and scantily clad models, (my wife knows I wouldn't even notice these!) hyping some of them. When you mention bedding at a show like this, people think you're talkin' about sheets and comforter covers!

But what they found were beds employing the "... same Pocketed Coil innerspring system found in the company's factory assembled mattresses". They claim assembly would take about five minutes. The coils are condensed in a vacuum wrap and spring to normal size "... when the second of two plastic wrappers is removed." Then you simply set up "... the bolster and bottom portion of the cover, lay the rows of coil inside and zip on the top cover". Voila, a bed!

Storing it after use is also a snap! (Or so they say!) The coils are placed back in the bag and you attach a vacuum cleaner that sucks out the air. This compresses the coils so that they fit back into the carton.

And I was goin' to be after tellin' the wife about this wonderful new bed but she'd just say: "Sure and you're still daft from when those leprechauns tripped you last St. Patty's day 'cause you wasn't a'wearin' the green!" She sure talks funny!

HAVE
MATTRESS
WILL
TRAVEL
MATTRESS
INSIDE
?

March 23, 1997

A TANTALIZING TABLE TALE!

What's 45 inches wide and about 8 1/2 feet long when it's just sitting around doin' nothin' and grows to about 15 1/2 feet long when it's fully extended? Don't know? Well, lemme tell you, it's a dining table that we've been carrying in stock and it's taken the town by storm!

I don't usually toot our horn unless I do it generally for the furniture industry but with the response to this number I just had to tell you what an absolutely wonderful item it is!

Of course at this size it's not just another dining table. It's got a triple pedestal base with a total of ten legs (go figure that one out!) and six leaves. It comes crafted in four major woods; Cherry, Oak, Mahogany and Walnut, about ten standard finishes plus a variety of 'custom' finishes.

The styling is Eighteenth Century Queen Anne which is our number one favourite and thus blends with so many accent pieces made specially to enhance this charming design.

We had it displayed only one way, as a closed table in Cherry, but fortunately we now also have an Oak version fully extended and it really takes your breath away!

The Oak collection is displayed with Queen Anne splat back side chairs and two matching arm chairs plus a pair of coordinating upholstered 'hostess' chairs that can be used in the living room as well. The Cherry version is shown with a more detailed splat back chair featuring a ball and claw leg. Fully extended this table seats 18 to 20 people comfortably.

However, there is a terrible down side. If you sit at one end of the table and your 'lovely' spouse at the other, you'd be absolutely too far away from her to hear all the vital, necessary and most important instructions that you normally must attend to all through dinner! And I wish to here and now, dispel the vile rumour that this is the main reason we have one of these beauties at home!

A TABLE FOR ALL SEASONS

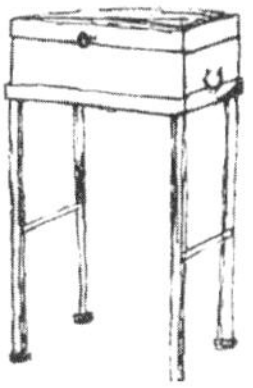

April 13, 1997

CURL UP WITH A CUBAN! (cigar that is!)

Cynthia, hold your nose honey and call me "RUSH" (Limbaugh that is) 'cause your man is a-gonna' be takin' up ceeegar smokin'!

With the advent of cigar smoking by such celebrities as the above mentioned "Rush", muscle man Arnold Schwarzenegger and the gap-toothed David Letterman, not to mention some pretty sexy ladies like Demi Moore, the cigar has moved away from its reputation as the seedy extension of bookies and crooked politicians (both fictional characters of course!). It is now considered a worthy accompaniment of, and get this Cindy, "... today's upwardly mobile, often conspicuous consumer". They sure 'nough got me pegged!

And it just so happens that we're goin' to a trade show this week and some of the exciting sneak previews that came in the mail are dealing with a hot new accessory and furniture item - Humidors.

To those of you unfamiliar with them, a humidor is a cedar-lined box that will store your cigars at a constant humidity. That way they'll stay fresh and smell good. (Real good!)

To meet the demands of today's new breed of cigar aficionados, humidor makers are offering a whole new range of these former staid cigar containers. You'll still be able to get the usual tried and true 'boxy' styles, but the manufacturers have hired top designers who have produced some new and beautiful pieces that are not only functional, but will make beautiful accessory items.

Because cigars and cognac and fine wines and spirits also, go together almost as well as my wife and her Visa card, furniture makers thought it would be a good idea to make tables that not only contain a built-in humidor, but also has provisions for a decanter and glasses. Voila, the advent of "Cigar Furniture"!

My wife once told me that if I 'ever' took up cigar smokin' she'd leave. I'm sure gonna miss you Honey!

Functional Furniture for sophisticated Cigars!

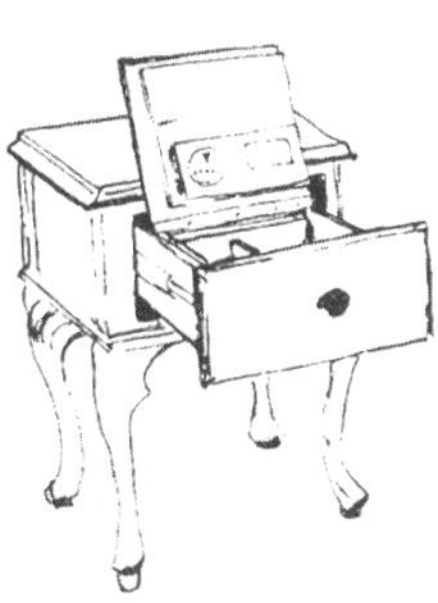

April 20, 1997

WE ALSO SHOP!!!

Last Wednesday we flew to the High Point Furniture Market in North Carolina. We arrived at night when everything was pitch black and didn't see the light of day till the mornin' when we were on the shuttle bus heading to market. From there we clambered on board another shuttle and were on our way to the Thomasville Furniture showrooms.

We were let off in the parking lot. Something looked funny to me but I couldn't put my finger on it. The lot was full of gleaming cars and they looked fine but there was an unreal surreal feeling to the place. Then it hit me. They were all clean!!!

We had left Winnipeg in it's normal slushy gray springtime cloak and arrived in an area where cars and people weren't in continual danger of being covered in that same slushy gray springtime mantel!

At showtime, when you're not visiting a manufacturer's showroom or plant you're probably attending the market in the city of High Point. There are several outlying buildings but the main show is in a huge building where there are scads (that means lots and lots dear) of displays, some of them being very huge in very large showrooms. It is also a building where I get continually and perpetually lost as do lots of other people. This year however, in the used-to-be Sears parking lot by the main building, a humungous tent was erected which housed many exhibits, in fact, scads of them! It was very easy to find where you were at all times and it was bright and airy. We went to the main building to buy three gorgeous lamp lines and spent the rest of the time in the tent, or at other showrooms. I loved it! Besides the fun of the big tent what really made this market relaxing for me was that my wife couldn't use her Visa card on this shopping spree!

TO MARKET, TO MARKET...

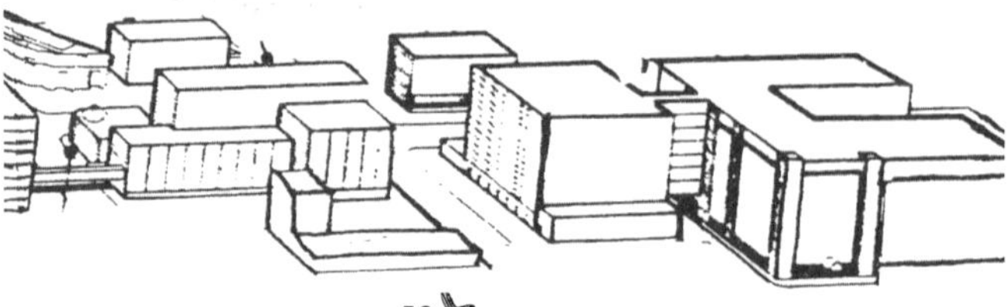

May 4, 1997

WATER, WATER, WATER!

Put another sandbag on,
On the Dike that's nearly gone,
All we got in Winnipeg,
Is Water, Water, Water.

This was part of a ditty sung and I believe composed by a terrific local band leader, the late Marsh Phimister and a group during the '50 flood. It was sung to the tune of a hit by Teresa Brewer titled Music, Music, Music and it sure stirred a lot of memories when I heard it played this week on our venerable, vital and vunderful (that's right, vunderful!) CBC radio!

I remember the '50 flood and the trauma we all went through. Four of us were living in a tiny apartment and the river was roughly a block away at the bottom of a hill; only it wasn't at the bottom anymore! It rose daily through April and early May. Water was seeping into the basement of the apartment building. It was very scary.

A gang of four or five of us cocky youths went sandbagging during the day and strutted like "Big Shots" through Winnipeg in the evening. One of the areas we sauntered through was where we now have our store and a lot of this area was under water!

One of the most poignant stories I heard about the '50 flood was of a ten year old girl who was home alone one day in early May. Both her parents worked and being alone made her even more acutely aware of the high-water threat. (There was a boat dock outside her house!)

Suddenly she heard a noise from the basement. Going to the top of the stairs she saw water entering the home through a crack in the basement wall. She slammed the door and called her Mom who rushed home. When I first heard the story I wished I could have been there to protect her. I've been trying to do just that for over 35 years. Sometimes I don't do so good but I still like to keep trying. You see I married that little girl!

May 11, 1997

THE DITCH THAT DUFF BUILT

PANAMA-BY-THE-RED

I was watching Larry Desjardins on TV the other night and he said something like: "I voted against the project, we all thought it was too expensive ..."

And then he mused that he and other naysayers were wrong, it was the best thing for this city. What project you ask? "Our" Floodway, known locally (and warmly), as Duff's Ditch.

I'm as guilty as anyone else of criticizing the foibles of our politicians. Lord knows they give us ample fodder! But when they do good things, when they rise above the crowd and really put the public interest ahead of theirs, then we must give them their due. The pulling together of this community in the face of the onslaught of our "Flood-of-the-Century" is of heroic proportions but it has a parallel, the building of our Floodway. This giant ditch that entailed moving more earth than it took to build the Panama Canal, required two feats of epic proportions, the second being the actual construction. The first was the foresight, vision and tremendous courage of the young politician who made it happen.

And I did say politician! The word stirs some unsavory connotations today but for me the Right Honourable Dufferin Roblin imparted to the word a sense of statesmanship and tremendous courage.

Can anybody just imagine what it must have entailed to keep moving ahead with a project of such mammoth proportions in the face of what must have been severe opposition? In spite of the adversity, he put Winnipeg and Manitoba first.

And if even a few homes get flooded it's still a tragedy but I dread to think how much worse it could have been without "Duff's Ditch"!! And not only now. Think of all those times in the past when most of us didn't even realize that the "Ditch" had quietly saved us from other hazardous times and tragedies.

There's a cute expression about getting off your so-called "duff" and doing something. Duff did!

May 18, 1997

COLOUR YOUR WORLD EXCITING!!

We're adding our last available four thousand feet of main floor space to our Thomasville Home Furnishings Store. It wasn't exactly 'rough' space but it needed renovation.

We've renovated many areas of our showroom so this would be fairly simple for us. Draw out the space, figure where the walls and electrical stuff goes, order carpet, do a colour scheme and then let 'er rip! The first "brawl" developed when the girls emptied the room without first having our renovation sale.

The second "set-to" occurred when I noticed that the exterior wall being drywalled was not being insulated. My wife said the cost would be prohibitive, this from the woman who will buy an "extra" microwave oven at the drop of a hat! I got a half-victory on that one, we insulated eight feet up the wall.

The third "shock" to my system came when, driving my errant son home one day he remarked on the red wall being painted at the back of the area! I don't know whether this was just casual conversation or whether he wanted to see his father get apoplexy! "Red wall!" I puffed "Red Wall!" I frantically phoned the office. Yep, without a word to me or my dog Roxy, the girls had decided on a bold colour scheme starting with the back room being Brick Red! (much like I was at that point!!)

I objected. My wife said: "We wanted to surprise you. Wait'll it's finished, you'll love it!"

I now understand the emotions customers go through when designers tell them at times to use strong colours and they have a very real fear that it 'just ain't gonna work'.

However, intense colours used properly can create a great deal of excitement and the comments of customers who have availed themselves of this feature is assurance enough that our space will turn out to be as exciting as some of the work we've done. (At least that's what my wife told me to say!)

WE GOT IT ALL FOR YOU!

June 8, 1997

BOUDOIR BIGGIES!

First it was beds, not the mattresses and stuff but the actual bedstead, the headboard and Footboard. What am I talking about? In a word, size.

Once upon a time when you bought a poster bed the posts were of a size that a normal person could put his hands around. Today however if you ain't a member of the Chicago Bulls there's no way you're getting your mitts around the newest offerings in bed posts. They're big and gettin' bigger!

Then of course night stands had to increase in size if they didn't want to look absolutely silly beside these gargantuan beds. I know many night stands intimately and they sure don't want to look silly, so they got bigger!

And now it's chests. Triple dressers usually had the option of a medium or a bigger size but chests seemed to be groping trying to find the proper size for the bedroom.

We had Armoires and some of these were pretty big but it got confusing when some manufacturers started calling normal size chests armoires and it was downhill from there on.

Today there's no messin' around, a large chest is really a large chest and even better, most are darn good lookin'!

There's always the chance that something that size could even have a certain vulgarity to it but of the ones I've seen, this has not happened. "They're large and in charge"! They're quite outstanding and the storage capacity and possibilities take your breath away. At last ..."A place for everything." And now, while we hate to toot our own horn (Oh yeah!) I can't help but mention that we'll soon be getting in some large chests (and accessories too!!!) from Mexico and they're absolutely magnificent! No doubt about it, they lack the finishing touches of our normal goods but this only enhances them more!

But back to those big, bad bedroom boxes (chests), I told my wife we needed more size in the bedroom. She lifted her eyes upward and muttered amen? Was that yes or no?

Chest Choices

June 22, 1997

MORE THAN A MARATHON!

I never attended a Manitoba Marathon. A buddy of mine used to do lots of work for this event but he never pressed me to attend, he knew I had better things to do on a Summer Sunday morning.

This year however a couple of his friends asked me to assist in a minor capacity. I weakened and showed up at the U of M stadium this past Sunday AM. Even though my job was small the greetings and the camaraderie made me feel part of a happening that seemed to be growing in importance by the minute.

Bout 7:00 AM I was asked by a group of people if I wanted to watch the runners 'take off.'

We walked over and stood on a grassy area between the full Marathoners and the half Marathoners.

The sound system was great and the music uplifting. It was hard to stand still.

Starting time was approaching. 10 minutes to go. The runners were massing at the starting line. 10 minutes quickly dissolved to 5 minutes and then one. Suddenly the music from "Chariots of Fire" hit the airwaves and the excitement was overwhelming.

The starter's pistol barked and the Marathoners took flight.

It blew me away. What a feeling. The initial relay runners were with the Marathoners, many continuing with the run after they passed the baton.

The 10 kilometer walkers were back of the runners and the 2.6 mile "Super Run" was to begin in 2 stages, at 7:10 and 7:20. This was an event for everyone and what a wonderful way for a family to kick-off Father's Day or just be together!

Going back to my post I spotted a sign along the way designating "Irv's Mile" This was my buddy and I hadn't known he was going to be honoured in this manner. He had died two years ago.

I just had to go up and touch "his" sign.

I muttered: "Hi Irv." He was a most wonderful friend and I miss him terribly but I never realized everyone else felt the same way!

The Manitoba Marathon

July 13, 1997

Shipping Stories and Truck Tales

We have a problem with freight. When stuff we buy leaves the factory destined for our shop, it becomes ours. The factory does not own it any more and the freight companies are just the delivery guys bringing it to us. For all intents and purposes, even though it's thousands of miles away, it's ours!

And when we sell goods to a customer the same thing follows, it's theirs. A lot of our sales are shipped to out of province locations and once it's picked up by the trucking firm it belongs to the customer.

End of story? Not really, you see there's a little thing called Damage In Shipping, only it ain't no little thing, it's a big, big headache!

Say you're a customer and you receive goods in a damaged condition. What do you do? Usually you call the store where you purchased the goods and complain. That's OK if the store shipped it in that condition, but I don't know many stores that would do that.

At our place and many others I'm sure, most items we sell are scrutinized (that means gone over real careful dear) and "deluxed" before leaving our dock.

Sometimes we slip up and Andy our "Magic Man" (just ask him!) has to make a service call.

But when goods go out of town, there ain't no way we're going to send Andy to Vancouver, Toronto or Saudi (yes we ship to Saudi!), everything's gone over special careful (yes dear, scrutinized!)

So when a customer reports damage to us, we tell him to save the carton and packaging material and contact the carrier. That's what must be done. Before anything else, the carrier must be contacted and notified of the damage. After this, if the customer requests it, we will help them through the claim procedure so that hopefully, the item will either be replaced or repaired to their satisfaction.

It's a thankless task and gets relegated to the lower echelons to perform, like husbands, who, if they're smart enough, dilly-dally around so long that their wives take over.

Works for me!

Keep on Truckin!

July 20, 1997

The Joy of Working! (Really!)

For me some of the most delightful times I've spent working are the people I've worked with. One of the most memorable people that shared "the floor" with us was a chap name of Lloyd. (He's very unassuming so I'm not going to use his last name.)

When he came to us he had recently been retired from a major department store in town but just wasn't ready to lay back and take it easy. In fact I suspect that was the last thing Lloyd wanted to do! He looked a lot younger than his 65 years and if you didn't stop him he would be helping the shippers lift furniture and move it around the showroom.

Lloyd was a Second World War fighter pilot but never noised it around. A quiet, gentle man, I could just visualize him getting the job done 'over there' and then returning home when it was finished properly. He was the kind of guy that never sat around idle or spent a lot of time chatting at the water cooler or sitting on a sofa. Instead, if there was no one in the showroom, he would be dusting furniture or straightening out displays. Everybody worked when Lloyd was around, you just couldn't help it! I mean how could you just sit around and do nothing when this 'so-called' older gentleman, (and he was every inch a gentleman) would be working steadily and without fanfare.

After many years Lloyd finally did retire but he still pops in occasionally with his charming wife. There's still a spring in his step and his appearance belies his years. My wife noticed it and said: "I don't know how he does it, he's older than you and still looks younger!"

I told her that all us furniture guys just keep getting more youthful.

She looked at me and said: "Right on!" Then she must have thought of something funny 'cause she began laughing real hard.

August 10, 1997

The Return of the Little Guy!

It's the middle of a hot Winnipeg August evening. You'd like a nice cold juicy peach. Sound good? You betcha! So, run down to your corner Mom and Pop operation and treat yourself. Only it ain't there anymore! It hasn't been for a number of years since the big chains exploded into our venue.

Instead you gotta run down to the chain and stand in line for a while and a while longer and you get your piece of fruit, only it's kinda warm and maybe a little pricey. Or you can run to that numbered convenience store. The produce is prepackaged and may look okay but to me it don't taste too exciting.

How about if you need something in hardware? Your local one has all kinds of good stuff and an owner that can tell you how to use them. Only both him and the store are gone, replaced by a giant impersonal emporium.

There's one near our house where finding merchandise is for me, a descent into madness! Information is available if you have lots of time and instructions on use can be non-existent. (I don't work in that department, Sir!!)

This lack of smaller stores is felt nowhere as greatly as in the furniture business.

Consumers are getting fed up with the same old furniture being "hawked" with the same old ads. Instead of creating excitement they've become so impersonal and boring! Or the opposite extreme, noisy and offensive! How many times can you hear the same old message without being completely turned off?

People are hungry to shop in a store where they can get something unique and different, something that hasn't been advertised to death.

I told my wife that customers want to be lured into a shop with" ... a mix of value and romance ... that can't be duplicated by ..." those large chains.

She looked at me and called out to my daughter, "Lisa, get Dad a cold peach!" She just don't get it!

August 24, 1997

Furniture With Salsa (Ole!)

Pssst, amigo, wanna buy some Meh-I-can furniture? Well, we got some!

I've done a couple of articles on Mexican furniture just to let you know of new, exciting style trends and construction. Just a little bit of furniture chit-chat and everyone, (well maybe a few people anyway) got mad at me 'cause we had none to show you. Well get unmad(!) 'cause we got some! Our head designer is wild about them and my wife apologized for giving me "what for" when buying them! The months of waiting are forgotten and the only regret is that we didn't buy more!

At the April show this year, the main Mexican exhibits were housed in a huge old building along with a multitude of other displays, most of them in areas which are quite open, giving one the impression of being at a large bazaar or, as my wife said, a huge flea market!

Most of the Mexican displays were housed at the rear of one of the upper floors. The massive pieces of furniture struck you first. They were crafted in pine, oak and other woods and were displayed sitting alone or stacked with such items as hand-blown glass pieces and stone pottery.

Some of the glass pieces were trimmed with metal and their shapes, type of glass used and colors were quite unique and exciting! As for the pottery (and stone fishes!), they really grabbed your attention! Some stuff was as rough and crude as a lot of the furniture but like the wood, some items were of a gentler hand.

And the people - zesty and full of life! My wife wandered off to other exhibits and let me do the Mexican purchases. When she came back I was talking to a lusty young lady (about furniture of course!) when I heard my name mentioned in a not-too-quiet voice. My Mexican adventure drew to a close. My wife though must have been fond of this young senorita also 'cause she hasn't stopped talking about her all year!

Hasta La Vista Baby

September 7, 1997

The Fall - Hay, Sowbugs and Gourds

I don't know how you feel about it but when I hear the weather guy or gal say it's going to be another gorgeous day of sun and 30 degree weather I think they're nuts! I'd much rather have the temperature hover in the low 20's with the odd cloud drifting by to give some shade; that 30 degree stuff is for muscle guys and bikini clad girls. So to me, the fall season is just about perfect; warm days, cool nights, even putting on the odd fire and ripe tomatoes on the vine. Yummy!

One of my favourite fall fun things is to cast maple and ash tree seeds, (aka "helicopters") into the air and watch the gleam on young (and not so young) faces as they gently float to earth.

And I love going to the markets and roadside stands at this time to pick up vegetables, herbs and fresh flowers. You can also get gorgeous dried arrangements now. I am sent out on this delightful mission and have a ball picking up these accessories for the shop. (and for home too!!)

Other tremendous accessories to adorn your room and especially your dining table are those colourful gourds. Like people, they're all different shapes and sizes! There's tall ones and squat ones. Some are smooth skinned while others have warts! A few have stripes while others are solid coloured and some are even bi-coloured! But most of all they're just delightful!

One year for a Fall display I outdid myself and procured (is this the right word?) two bales of hay. They were brought inside when we were ready to set up our Fall display. However, unbeknownst to us, a "Sowbug" hotel had opened for business in the hay bales and these little varmints went scurrying around amid the screams of my wife and other assorted personnel.

Afterwards my wife said (in an uncalled for tone!): Next time you bring display adornments inside, leave your buddies outside!

September 14, 1997

The Road Warriors!

I promised my wife I'd behave and write about furniture this week but there is an absolutely burning issue that I must render into script before I burst!

Recall if you will, the cloning of sheep and other marvelous (?) experiments in genetics. Well, they didn't all go smooth, there were mistakes and I've discovered how they've hidden those "results" that didn't turn out so well. I stumbled, or rather cycled upon them while riding my bike to work in the early morning hours.

You see, the scientific experiments have left these "results" with a cunning that allows them to behave normally most of the time, but hidden behind the wheel of a car their black side emerges and the sight of a cyclist enrages them!

To prolong their blood sport they don't destroy these cyclists but take pleasure in coming very close to their prey at wonderful speeds, leaving them in a state of mortification. Another wonderful tool in their repertoire is the use of hand signals, some being quite interesting, while others seem to be dredged up from a Neanderthal past.

These at times actually precipitate a cyclist falling off his craft as he is overcome by the terrible burden suffered by the motorist in trying to secure enough brain and eye coordination to make these complex (?) hand gestures!

And if this isn't enough challenge to the poor cyclist, others allied to these frenzied drivers and suffering similar cranial disorders, wait in parked vehicles till the "bikes" are very close then either pull out sharply or just open the vehicle door!

I have enough work just staying on my bike without these jockeys toying with me. In fact 'bout two years ago I took a goodly tumble all by myself. When I came into work the next day after 6 hours in emergency, bruised, battered and with an ear very large and swollen, my adoring designer said: "Oh, how did you get to work? Did you fly?"

Fine Furniture, Tired Bones ...

September 21, 1997

Facts of Life (Retail Style!)

Fact #1: Autumn officially begins somewhere near 7:00 PM Monday, September 22nd.

Fact #2: It's mid-September and the nights are getting a bit chilly, some even bein' downright cold!

Fact #3: My wife again told me how tired she was this morning. I don't know why, all she did last night was eat supper, in a restaurant yet!

Now here's a few more that are even more important:

Fact #4: Us furniture dealers have been pretty good in not praying for rain on the weekends (Well maybe the odd weekend).

Fact #5: We gave you a gorgeous Summer (forget about Spring) and an even gorgeouser Fall.

Fact #6: Summer's over and your indoor entertainment and family togetherness season is nigh.

Where's all this leading? Simple. For goodness sakes, get back indoors and start playing house! How long do you think we furniture guys are goin' to give you before we start with the funny weather? We got connections up there where it counts, no brag, just fact!

We're all sitting around loaded with great merchandise at super prices while you all frolic in the great outdoors, sopping up the delicious Summer that was and the sumptuous Fall that is.

Enough already! For your information, you've just about blown your chances to order a dining suite for this Fall! Don't wait till November or December to order one for Christmas or Chanukah! And if a bedroom suite is in the offing the same rules apply! At this time of year inventories start being gobbled up and if you don't get your orders in soon you'll be calling me in January to see if your December order will get here for Valentine's day in February!

So put away the boats and frisbees, the kites and water skis and start thinking warm indoor nights by the fire and enjoying all that fabulous new furniture!

PS As for fact #3, my wife actually does make supper and we eat at home every single night (except Monday, Tuesday, Wednesday, etc. etc.!).

October 5, 1997

Fun and Games with Furniture!

I generally moan about people spending too much time and money (especially money!) on unimportant things like TV's, computers, cars and other such trivia and not enough on essential stuff like furniture.

It seems that the reasons the furniture industry is fighting a losing battle for its share of consumer spending is that we're losing the war for our share of the consumer's leisure time.

Today's consumer is more affluent and has more free time or at least makes more leisure time for themselves and the challenge to manufacturers and retailers alike is, can we add meaning and fun, yes fun, to your leisure time?

This is a real problem, Nothing we sell tastes good. We got no chairs with horns on them to make my mother-in-law happy or no sofas that can hit 60 kilometres per hour in six seconds to make my young son grin. There are toss cushions with scenes embroidered on them and some wooden furniture has scenery or portraits painted on them. But they don't move or talk and you can't change the pictures by clicking a remote!

At a recent Furniture Association convention in San Diego, the keynote speaker, Mr. Watts Wacker, known as a futurist who examines the impact of social, economic, political and technological changes on consumer buying behavior says that consumers are looking for "a lot of their satisfaction, fulfillment and meaning of life outside work."

Our industry's job therefore is to educate the consumer to the fact that furniture can add fun and meaning to leisure time.

We've got to teach people that staying at home can be as meaningful as a vacation, and buying furniture can be as much fun as buying another gadget.

So I explained this to my wife and she said, "Great! Why don't we take home that gorgeous new Renaissance Collection dining suite and the exquisite Elysee Collection bedroom suite and tell everybody what fun we're having!?"

Leapin' lizards, I hope she's only kidding!

October 12, 1997

The Market, Books and Tony!

As a kid I never read much, just getting through the day at school was enough problem without reading other books. Mom and Dad read voraciously and my sister was always buried in a book. My brothers hit only the sports pages and the comics, especially the Comics. As for myself, I just did the comics, period.

But somewhere in my early teens I acquired a pocket book murder mystery and I was hooked! Like my sister, I took to this genre with an appetite that would not be sated. I read all comers from Ellery Queen to Agatha Christie but I was particularly fond of Perry Mason and Nero Wolfe mysteries, with a leaning towards Nero, the "Fat Man" and his passion for orchid gardening.

And of course, once I got my hands on the Sherlock Holmes collection I was lead into other worlds and adventures by Sir A. Conan Doyle.

Now, I rarely have time to scan the newspaper let alone peruse my favorite journals which my wife threatens to discard saying that the top of my night table resembles a magazine graveyard!

But I'll be reading a new book called "Killer Market" by Margaret Maron. It's a murder mystery that takes place at the High Point Furniture Market where I'll be in 10 days! The book means a lot to me. I received it by mail from a "furniture friend" name of Tony Spinola who doesn't forget birthdays either! It reminds me that besides the gruelling work schedule of a market there is the camaraderie of those special people that you might only see once or twice a year.

They're kindred spirits and it's nice to "go home again" and visit for awhile.

And the guys do you real favours. They tell my wife how terrible the shopping is at the malls this year so my wife won't have to bother running around for anything personal. Sometimes she even listens!

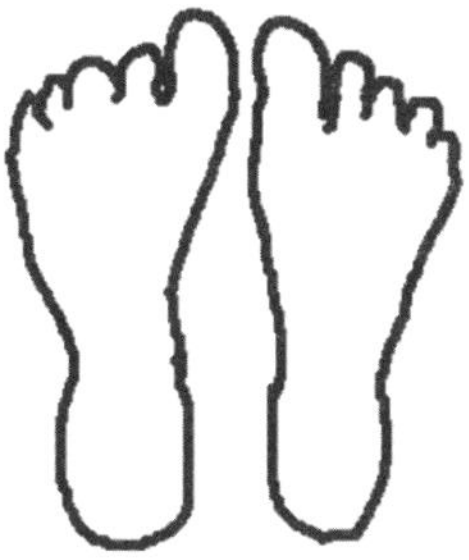

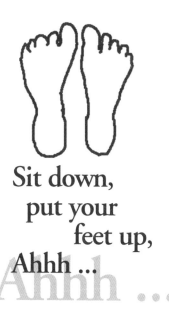

Sit down,
put your
feet up,
Ahhh ...

Ahhh ...

November 30, 1997

BABY IT'S COLD OUTSIDE!

Forget about the cost of wood these days or having to lug it in from the garage or the woodpile outside the house. And forget about the ashes later on, they're a cinch to sweep up and take out and they're tremendous sprinkled in the garden as a source of phosphorous and to keep the slugs in check.

Because there's nothin' cozier than cuddlin' up in front of a wood fireplace on one of our crisp, frosty, January evenings. If there is, I ain't heard of it yet!

And while the genuine article is quite nice there's some pretty 'nifty' "faux" fireplaces and mantles out there that can give the real ones a run for their money!

They're not only great looking, they've become a fixture in a lot of furniture stores. They really add a dimension and warmth to a room setting. They've also become a tremendous sale item at most furniture stores!

We bought four different models and they've really generated a lot of excitement on our floor!

We have one displayed in a sort of contemporary Shaker setting. It's in red brick (Hey, that's almost my name!) with two openings, one for the actual fireplace mechanism and the other for wood. The mantle is dark cherry and with the fireplace "on", it's very, very inviting!

In another model the entire mantle is done in a semi-gloss creamy ivory tone with traditional lines and motifs. The fireplace opening is large and we've placed andirons and a screen in front of the actual grill and faux logs.

It's also fully accessorized and is not only cozy and inviting, it's beautiful.

My wife has always wanted a real fireplace in the bedroom but the idea of trundling wood up to the second floor wasn't too appealing. So I told her that we could keep the real one downstairs and just fake it in the bedroom. She stared at me and burst out laughing. Now what on earth was so funny?

**C'mon Baby,
Light My
Fire...place!**

December 28, 1997

GIMME A BREAK!

How many times have you heard that old chap on the preview channel pitch his prearranged funeral plan? Don't you wish he was already using it? We've heard it so many times that the message has become garbled. My wife is confusing it with the message from that other old codger who, upon answering the telephone, reaches a state of unbridled ecstasy when his son at the other end, tells him that he's just purchased insurance! Wow, is that ever great! Imagine, insurance! I think I'll just buy some and rush to the phone and call Daddy!

"Hi Mom is Dad in? I've got grrrreat news for him, I just bought INSURANCE!!!!! Whazzat Mom? Dad's not there anymore? He was so delighted with his prearranged funeral that he decided to use it early? Well good for him!"

This prearranged funeral tirade seems to play at least 10 times an hour whenever I'm scanning the preview channel. I thought this type of repetitious pitching was forbidden by the CRTC but I guess I was wrong.

You'd think the people running the preview channel would have a little more sensitivity for us couch potatoes but I guess business is business.

I think we pay enough for the cable service without being bombarded so mercilessly just tryin' to find out what's on TV!

But I'm afraid most other industries, if given the chance, would also do the same as these guys if they could. In fact my own industry, the furniture business, is one of the worst culprits as far as aggressive advertising goes. And right behind us are the car dealers (and manufacturers!). It's not that the ads are so bad, in fact some are even quite good but the mind-numbing frequency is what drives me nuts.

I told my wife about this. She said: "I know how you feel, I really do! I know. I know! They really drive me crazy too. I know how you feel. I really do. I know, I know, I know ..."!

January 4, 1998

SHIPPING AND RECEIVING!

One of the most exciting times for me in the furniture business is when a semi pulls up to our back door with anywhere from 80 to 200 pieces on board! All of a sudden the place just shifts into high gear! The guys go outside to help guide the truck as he backs up to our loading dock, our doors swing open and we bring out the wooden or metal "plate" to bridge the gap between the truck's rear end and our door.

Then, the driver rolls up his rear door and in we go. We have a list of what's on board made up by our office manager David. The upholstered pieces are usually bigger and more awkward and these get shunted into their own area so as to leave room for the wooden stuff. Dining chairs are packed two to the box, they're big, but stackable.

We also separate the "tag" orders, those that belong to customers. These get priority treatment!

Time was when I used to help the guys unload the trucks. They actually put up with the "old man" at the dock and would only drop the occasional dresser on him!

I still remember the 220 piece shipment that came in on a Friday night that wasn't supposed to hit here till Monday. It was a real Manitoba Winter, not any of this "El Nino" sissy stuff and the driver just wanted to "dump" the load as fast as he could and get back to southern climes!

There was to be a shipper on that night but he left early. I told Cindy that I'd give the driver a hand, but I unloaded it myself.

When it was over she took one look at me and said: "You did it alone." She really was concerned. Now when I mention that 220 piece shipment (and I rarely do!), she says: "If I hear that story again I'll kill myself!" She lies.

No dead weight here...

January 18, 1998

COLD PIZZA AND OLD FRIENDS - THE TORONTO FURNITURE SHOW

We went to the Toronto Furniture Show!

This was not a voluntary process!

The wife and I weren't going to the show. 'Cause maybe we'd take a little holiday instead. I've said many times, a trip to a furniture show sure ain't no holiday and I needed one?

However fate interceded. My wife, while engaged in one of her "marathon" chats with the designers, let it slip that maybe we wouldn't be goin' to the show!

We're in a big building. I was maybe 100 feet away but I heard the screech!

"You're not going to the show?!! Do you know how busy we've been?! Do you realize what we're out of?! "All this in an octave above the lunch break whistle at a steel plant, "And you're not going to the show?! You were trying to sneak this past us weren't you?! You weren't going to tell us till after?! And on and on ... So, we went to the show.

This was Tuesday and we leave by Saturday.

We booked our flight and hotel the next day and my daughter Marsha bought me apples. She knows that when I travel I munch a lot of apples.

My prime concern was to see a chap selling tapestries. I saw him last year but couldn't make it back to his booth. He didn't show. I next wanted to see the firm selling Brazilian soapstone carvings. Not there either.

But we finally bought some good stuff such as accessories from a Tunisian chap. One of the pieces was a beautiful domed birdcage in white with soft blue accents. He said it's from an area on the Mediterranean where everything is done in blue and white. He said it's restful and beautiful. Judging by the birdcage, he's right!

Some people might think I don't enjoy being with my wife 24 hrs a day at the show. What nonsense! Why I've even booked the next show in advance already, sometime in the year 2020!

To Market,
To Market!

February 1, 1998

IN THE BEGINNING ...

It was a dark and stormy night and chilly and windy too. Rain was pelting our windows and heightening our anxiety. We knew something big was gonna happen but we didn't know what.

It was a good time to be indoors. We were in our first store location, a second floor walk up on a one-way street going the wrong way, a real, prime location.

Suddenly the staircase creaked. Somebody was coming and breathing hard. He seemed to walk purposefully up those bending stairs with one strong step and then a weaker one. "He's got a limp" my wife said showing off her training as General George Custer's scout at the massacre of Little Big Horn. We looked at each other, fear written on our visages (and faces too!) and for what seemed an eternity we waited for the stranger to appear.

He finally did. A man of average height, wearing a topcoat that had seen better days and probably a few nights. He was carrying something large and heavy in his right hand. We were frozen with fear not knowing what was coming next when he uttered those fateful words, "Hi there, I'm the Thomasville salesman for this area."

His name was Arvid Wilson and he truly was one of the finest people I've ever met. We both drank Cutty Sark Scotch and loved Chinese food and hit it off just dandy! He couldn't open an account for us unless we ordered minimum $5,000.00 worth of furniture. Almost thirty years ago that was a lot of bread. We took the plunge and barely slept for the next three nights. We'd never spent that kind of money before and were we scared!

But Arv was in constant contact with us, "those two kids", he told somebody and we weren't gonna let him down!

That visit will always be with us in spite of the fact that neither of us (especially the wife) can remember where the toothpaste is each and every morning!

The day
Mr. T.
came to town

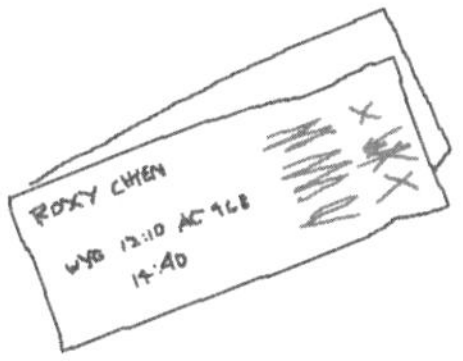

February 15, 1998

CHECK THOSE TICKETS!

Before flying I always check my airline tickets. I don't bother with seating 'cause my wife grabs the window seat anyway ... Once for a convention in Arizona we were having trouble getting a flight out. It was during a typical Winnipeg winter and everyone was heading south.

We contacted the supplier hosting the event and said: "HELP!" Voila, in three days we had tickets. I didn't even check them 'cause these people knew their business. We flew to Arizona leaving behind snow, cold, and a few bratty kids.

At the meeting we were kept busy from dawn till dusk. The evenings we spent meeting new dealers and renewing old friendships. On the last day we were to fly out around 5:00 PM and pick up a connecting flight out of Minneapolis to Winnipeg that same evening.

Cindy was lounging by the pool and I was running around looking at plants and stuff. Around 3:15 PM I told Cindy we better get ready to leave soon and I went to the room. I checked our tickets for the first time. Our flight was at 3:30 not 5:00!

I rushed to the "action" desk of the resort. They located a 4:30 flight to Minneapolis, got us to the airport by 4:10 and had us "fast tracked" to our flight!

In Minneapolis we missed our connecting flight by seven minutes and had to stay overnight at an airport hotel.

We got a bag with a toothbrush and not much else. We had no baggage. We snacked and retired to our room. I can't sleep without my "Jammies". My wife had a half-slip but I only had Jockey shorts. I eyed her half slip. She said "Forget it!" I said: "Halfers", this always used to work on my wife. "You get 'em from Midnight till two and I get 'em from two till morning" I said.

She snickered and said: "No deal! But when we get home I'll buy you your very own."

It was a very cold night.

Next trip I'll check my tickets.

February 22, 1998

AS CLEAR AS GLASS!

You know what the best thing about furniture markets are?

You probably think it's seeing all the new offerings or maybe all the travelling around (you can have it!). Or perhaps the buying. Viewing all the displays and buying what you need or what you think will be "hot" in the coming year.

Nah, while those things are important, the workload is usually so hectic you haven't time to do much else but scrutinize, buy or not buy and move quickly to the next stop 'cause time is at a premium and you better hustle.

The best time is actually being at the shop when a shipment arrives.

The wooden and upholstered pieces exude some sighs of delight, especially if it's something unique. For example, the curved desk from Thomasville, heavily antiqued and with "worn" leather inlays. It's not only unique, c'est très magnifique!

But the real squeals of joy come when the accessories arrive.

Sometimes they aren't all squeals of joy. At times when you unpack a shipment, some of the items make you wonder if you got too close to a skateboarder with a certain funny scent and your discerning eye was clouded, so to speak, but most times it's really a super feeling. You're back home and can enjoy these treasures in a comfortable setting without the frenzied pace of market. For instance, we bought some glass items this year that are just dazzling. From thick-sided triangle shaped containers to a bulky, round glass 'slab' perfect for cutting cheese on, or the tortoise shaped bowl in clear, chunky glass.

And do you know how hard it is to find a large, lucid, curved glass vase? Well I found one! It's an ample size and beautifully simplistic!!

And then there's the animals, but that's for another day.

I asked my wife if she noticed how many really odd pieces there were at the show this year.

"Uh-Huh" she said, "I brought one home."

Funny, I don't remember her buying anything.

Clearly Wonderful Accessories!

March 1, 1998

ANIMAL FARM, A LA BRICK'S!

Remember that old song that started with the line; "Have you ever seen a dream walkin'..."

Well I'm sure that we've all seen a "dream" walkin', sort of, but I bet you've never seen a cat or dog or even a cow fishin'! Well, I never did either until last summer when we received a shipment from a new accessory source. This year we not only repeated a shipment from that same supplier but also added another source to our suppliers list for this type of "fun" accessory.

So if you're walkin' by an armoire, curio cabinet or tall china in our showroom and you happen to look up, you may see a cat sitting on the edge of the furniture piece in a bent over position looking right back at you! We also got a pair of "swayback" (that's just a nice term for a belly that's scraping the ground!), haughty hogs that don't take no guff from nobody and a trio of two (one mysteriously wandered) proudly poised penguins not to mention a pair of upstart cocky roosters that look as proud as peacocks!

And if that ain't enough animals, somebody cut a cow in half and now we got a pair of bookends!

Another set of bookend features two felines with stunned looks on their faces who seem to be wondering how they got rooked into that job!

We also have two cats who want to fun all over the place and a trio of others who are so prissy they're above that sort of stuff and won't even look directly at you!

And then there's the ducks. We've been looking quite some time for carved waterfowl and these, while they don't evoke too many giggles, are an excellent accessory for a study or den.

My wife, looking over my shoulder said: "You didn't mention the five loons." "No more room" I said, "Besides, we only have four."

She gave me a long stare and said: "Five, and the fifth one does make you giggle." She never could count too well!

April 12, 1998

VOODOO STICKS AND CD RACKS!

It's a sealed bamboo "tube" about 40 inches long and 3 inches wide in a deep brown tone with black accents and gold painted dragons. Our invoice calls it a "Rain Stick" but our finisher Andy says his momma in New Orleans calls it a "Voodoo Stick".

The "Stick" is filled with beans and stuff and makes the most delicious rain sounds as you turn it slowly end to end. However Andy says that's not its real purpose. He says his momma would take it outside when it was raining and shake it 'bout three times and sometimes the rain would stop! Uh huh. It's part of an accessory shipment that we've just received and if you want a big "lift" (or even a big stick!) just stick around while an accessory shipment is being unpacked. (I really do apologize for the punnery, but it's so much funnery!)

Another fascinating item is the rectangular coffee table that ain't. It ain't 'cause it's actually a ladder! I'm sure these are in exotic import stores but I just had to have one.

It's solid teak and 18" x 32". It has an invisible seam in the middle that's hinged and when you lift one end it folds back onto the other side becoming a ladder. You'd better look at the picture!

And another item that's probably around town but I still had to have one, is our mini-teak CD stand. It's actually quite a cute item and resembles a spice or apothecary chest. When you open it, both sides swing out revealing space for scads of CDS and other stuff and, it ain't plastic!

I told my wife that the Voodoo stick has "called" to me to take time off to study other cultures. She said: "If the lessons don't include hangin' up your clothes and takin' out the garbage you'll have a lot more time on your hands than you bargained for!"

She just ain't got no mind for culture!

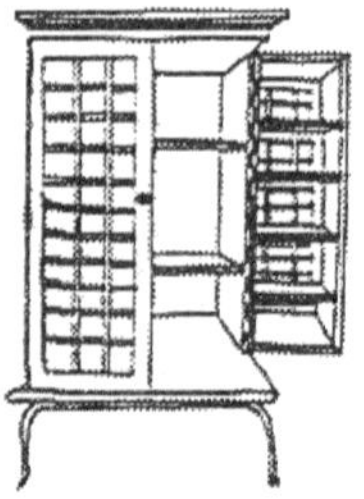

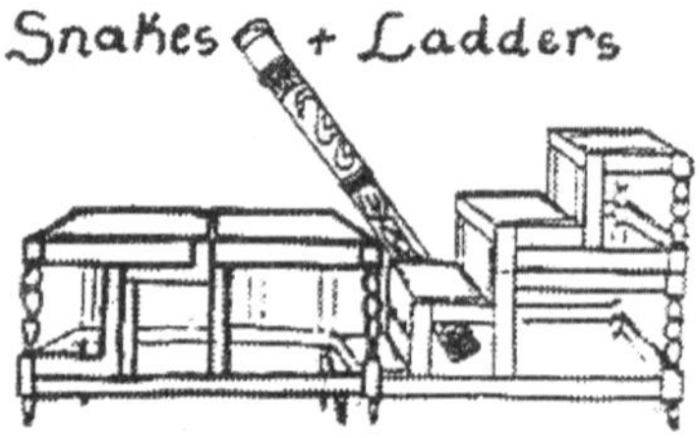

April 19, 1998

THE CURIOUS USE OF CURIOS!

Have you ever seen a "Tear Collector"? You mean you don't know what a tear collector is? Relax, I didn't either till my sister showed me one.

It's a tiny bottle or vial with a wee mite of a spoon that's used to collect and store the tears of a poor damsel immersed in sadness 'cause her Knight in shining armour is away at battle or visiting his mother or something. Because of its tiny size, you might be hard pressed to find a place to place this most interesting curio. Fortunately for my sister, she has a curio cabinet.

I keep thinking what a great idea curio cabinets are for the multitude of collectors out there. Very rarely now do you run into anybody that's not saving something very worthwhile to them.

The range of objects is as broad as anybody's imagination and there's no end to the collectable craze. I've seen some gorgeous collections from Swarovski crystal to antique china pieces, to doll collections. Some people specialize in animal groups and such diverse themes as pigs and Owls are especially prized.

With apartments and condos being quite miserly in the allocation of space for a dining room, we find there is oftentimes no room for a china cabinet. In these instances people opt for a curio cabinet to store their current china pieces. A lot of these curios have closed doors in the base which makes it ideal for concealed storage of tablecloths, napkins and knickknacks (or knickers!). I told my wife that whenever I'm going to be leaving for awhile I'll get her a tear collector and she can show me exactly how much she missed me.

"Better make it a large bottle" she said.

"Really?" I replied.

"Sure" she said, "Maybe a quart bottle, or a two litre jug. Maybe a gallon or a vat, yeah how about a vat?"

Sometimes she gets awful silly.

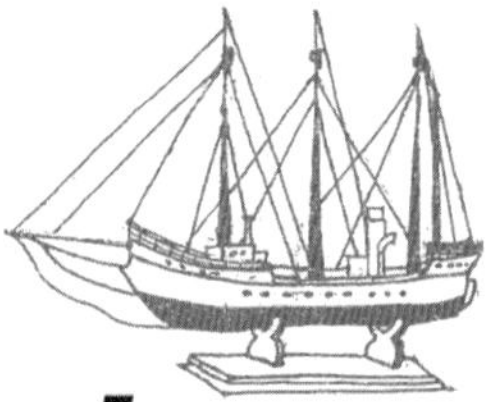

May 10, 1998

Rough Seize!

I've often mentioned that unpacking a new shipment of accessories can be one of the most exciting things we do at work. So when a new shipment arrived on Wednesday, I snuck to the back of the shop to "help" the boys unpack it.

Another reason for doing this is to make sure that all the stuff that arrives makes it to the showroom floor and out of a certain person's sticky fingers, which person shall go unnamed as long as she keeps her mitts off the goods, period.

This time however there was a greater hue and cry over a particular carved ship that arrived. My wife's radar picked up the message and she is now busy lobbying to get this singular item at home.

Further as Mother's Day was almost nigh, the pressure to charge this to our account and take it to our abode was fast mounting. However, nothing with my wife is ever that simple. Taking home this magnificent vessel would most assuredly entail trotting home assorted coordinating items to create a fantastic nautical ambiance.

She's really good at what she does! The ensuing debt she would give birth to would hinder me obtaining my necessities of life, namely garden manuals and computer games.

The last time that faraway glint appeared in her eye I had brought home a magnificent Oriental clock out of Portugal. This simple display of affection unleashed a heretofore bridled frenzy that began with us procuring an Oriental dining suite, a makeover of the living room including grass cloth and several Far Eastern items and finally spent itself on a striking Oriental bedroom suite. Though it turned out gorgeous, I told you she's good at what she does, I was not ready for another assault on my pocketbook, especially with the new Windows 98 on the horizon!

Besides, I already got her a Mother's Day gift hidden behind the loveseat in the study. And while it's not extravagant, who needs extravagance when she's got me?!

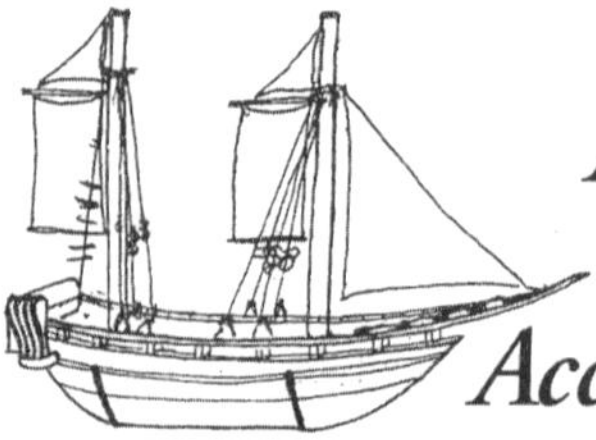

A Sea of Accessories

May 31, 1998

Packaging, Crating and "TLC"!

At one time or another we've all seen that comic routine where a cashier is checking out a customer's groceries and a young and not too bright chap (why is it always a guy!) is jamming food and other purchases into bags without too much care or caution 'cause his attention is focused on the pretty cashier.

Of course for comedic effect, the first thing into the bag are the eggs on top of which he cheerfully drops all the other merchandise. When the customer gets home he or she will have a few eggs and bits of shells ready for scrambling.

As is usual with comedy, somebody else's misery is our chance to laugh a bit. But it really ain't funny. Gettin' stuff delivered or bringing it home yourself and finding it damaged can be downright heartbreaking. Before stuff leaves our warehouse for local delivery, it's gone over really carefully although the odd time we slip up and hopefully we promptly try to service the customer.

But we ship a tremendous amount of merchandise across and out of Canada, even to Europe and other distant ports and we don't have finishers to service our clientele in Switzerland or Saudi so we have to be sure it leaves here in pristine condition and arrives that way! And we do!

The guys, Ray and Mike really know their stuff and construct a safe and solid container and everybody's "tickled pink"! We're happy 'cause we know the customer's gonna get merchandise in good shape. The customer's happy and even a bit shocked (we get letters!) that it arrived in such good shape and the transport carrier is happy 'cause there's no claim.

Somebody once remarked to me that we treat our furniture with TLC, "Tender Loving Care".

I told my wife that we're just like Nurses with our furniture, giving it lots of TLC. "Listen", she said, "you wanna treat the furniture fine, alright, but you better not start walkin' around the showroom in a white uniform and a perky cap!"

...Brown Paper Packages
Tied up with string...

June 7, 1998

Diamonds in the Rough

Many moons ago during the last world war, before my wife was born (Hah!), most kids were reading Superman and Captain Marvel comics, but my brothers and I were teething on Willie and Joe cartoons.

These were two luckless, dogfaces, (GI's), that went through the motions of being in the army and made the best of it.

In one of my favourite cartoons Willie and Joe were kneeling around a floating crap game while behind them stood a couple of other weary dogfaces.

Willie says to Joe: "Move over a bit more, they're comin' closer."

In other words, they were trying to lure "fresh blood" and money(!) into the game. I can hear my wife now: "What's this got to do with furniture?" Well, read on my dove and you'll find out.

Every year at this time we have to plant up 20 window boxes with 60 geraniums and 'bout 180 other assorted plants. There used to be plenty of help from "Les Girls", in fact they threatened to take over the complete operation!

But as of late, they've been too busy, so I had to "go fishing" for other "willing" helpers.

A couple of years back in desperation, I gently coaxed our two shippers, Willie and Joe, AKA Ray and Mike, to help me. While they're terrific shippers and even better packers, they had no gardening experience and I figured the operation was fraught with danger.

No way! They not only helped, they were eager to learn and the job went pretty smooth. Last year was even better, they not only helped in the planting, they made some suggestions which prettied up the planting. Not only that, we have a planting between our two rear loading docks which they tend and do a bang up job.

Now don't get me wrong, these are two rough and ready guys but it's amazing what you can find when you look deeper.

As my wife says when she talks about me, "When I found him he was nothing. Now, HE thinks he's something!"

July 5, 1998

Grout Ain't Good for Guys!

I don't know how many times we've all heard that "They don't make 'em like they used to". I think there are very few instances when this old adage can't be pulled out, dusted off and said with a voice bordering on concern and a visage akin to wisdom, if not brilliance.

There are even cases when it's true, one being about a coffee table constructed by hand by a future furniture retailer and his demure wife.

When we got married, a long time ago when the earth was young, we had little in the way of furniture and even less in the way of money. We bought a few rudimentary things like a mattress set, small bedroom suite, sofa and chair and kitchen suite but there was nothing left over for luxury items such as a coffee table.

A lifetime before, in second year maths, I had taken a fancy to a design in spatial geometry. I still can't draw worth a snit but I could replicate this design 'cause it was straight lines and I thought it quite beautiful. I bought a piece of three-quarter plywood, drew and cut out an oval table near five feet long using only a handsaw! Then, as I recall, we varnished or shellacked the surface and let it dry.

The spatial design was already drawn on the surface and following the pattern, we laid three different types of miniature ceramic tiles onto the table top. We then filled the spaces between the tiles with grout, washed off the excess and waterproofed the grout. We measured and screwed 4 hanger plates into the bottom to hold 4 legs et voila, c'était fini! (I sure hope Joanne my French teacher reads this!)

That darn table lasted us for years and may still be somewhere in the family!

I told my wife that they don't make stuff like that table or guys like me anymore. She said: "You're right, but we could always make the table look better with a new application of grout!"

July 12, 1998

The Bigger They Are ...!

Like most fashion manias at their peak, the four seater sofa probably seemed a great idea. But in hindsight, I marveled that people would bring something so encompassing into their quaint domains. They began at about 96 inches and units of 108 or more were not uncommon. When four people actually sat on them only the two on either end were comfortable. The two hapless souls in the middle had nowhere to put their hands, usually sitting clasping them in front like two school kids being punished!

And there was usually an oversized coffee table smacked down in front of this gem making it hard to get into and impossible to get out of your seat! What fun! And this was the good part yet! The nightmare of delivering this monolith was an exercise in patience and frustration! First of all, it was at least the height of most ceilings so to try and stand it on end to manoeuver it around a corner was near impossible. To get it up a staircase was a feat worthy of mention in the Guinness book of World Records.

In high-rises it would not fit in the elevator nor would they allow it to ride on top. We used to rent a crane to be placed on the top of a high-rise and swing the sofa in through the balcony! Or even better, if there was no balcony, a double window frame would be removed and it was swung in that-a-way! One adventurous couple, not wanting to hire a crane for the move out, hoisted their four seater down from the balcony on ropes. Unfortunately nobody took the time to measure. They were too short. The sofa fell 'bout 16 feet to the ground - and died!

"Remember those 4-seater sofas?" I asked my wife.

"Yes" she replied, "Weren't they wonderful! So roomy and spacious!"

"Yeah but delivering them ..." I began.

"Oh yes" she exclaimed, "Some said it was tough work but we had some wonderful adventures with them didn't we?"

"My very words" I muttered.

If three's a crowd, then four's a . . . ?

July 26, 1998

Of Tables and Tomatoes!

When we go grocery shopping, I buy the produce. Long ago at our house it was decided that Mother should keep out of the supermarket produce section unless accompanied by a member of the family, child or adult!

I should give some examples of what precipitated this harsh measure but I'd have to sleep with one eye open until these examples passed from the living memory of my spouse.

Mind you, it would only be for a day or two, memory not being a strong point amongst the adults in our family!

Now as much as we like to poke fun at Mom, I find that difficulty in selecting and buying good produce is not that uncommon. Now you may think it's a far stretch from fruit and vegetables to furniture but maybe not. They're both commodities that we purchase for our own use and both involve a "selection" process by us, the consumer. But that's around where the similarities stop. For instance if you make a mistake in produce selection you really haven't lost a lot of money and hopefully you'll learn by your mistakes and do better the next time. With furniture your error can be more costly and next time might be a long time comin'! So some of us furniture stores have interior designers on staff to assist you in selection, layout, colour and other important stuff. They're not going to push their own tastes on you, they'll just help select and coordinate the items that your tastes favour. To make their job and your choice easier, many stores, ours included, have furniture set-up in a home-like environment giving you a very realistic view of what your choices would or could look like in your own home.

Now if only we could get some produce managers to help customers pick out foodstuffs 'cause while my wife has become a pretty good designer, we still don't let her get anywhere near a produce counter alone!

While Visions of Sugarplums Dance in her Head ...

December 6, 1998

Jingle Bells Like Never Before!

It was the tackiest thing I'd ever seen, not to mention poor taste! I was at the drug store in our area (if you're zooming by car) last night when someone near me started singing "Jingle Bells" in a sort of pleasant baritone voice.

I turned but there was no one near me. Must be music over their store audio system I mused.

When I passed that aisle again the singing started which I thought was perhaps more than a coincidence.

The third time I saw him, "Bruce the Spruce", a singing Christmas tree!

When I got out to the car I couldn't stop laughing and had to explain to my curious companion, my adventures with, "Bruce the Spruce". She joined me in hearty laughter. She was dying to see "Bruce" but couldn't go in to the shop. This was a late night adventure and she was loosely clad in a fluffy nightgown, an open coat and boots, and she didn't want to frighten small children, but that's another story!

Now "Bruce" has nothing on the furniture industry. As far as tacky goes we've had some real gems ourselves!

For instance, I remember a sectional by a Canadian manufacturer that would have given "Bruce" a good run for his money! The round posts of the outside arms and two of the inner ones were actually "silos" that held, are you ready for this?, lamps!

Honest!

The arms had a small pin which you could push up and a table lamp would appear. Of course the cover for the "silo" was still attached so you had a lamp wearing what looked like, a very stupid hat!

It was a scream and even though it sold very well I just couldn't bring myself to put one on the floor. Heck besides being absolutely tasteless I couldn't stop laughing every time I saw it!

Now back to "Bruce". I chuckled the entire night and bought "Bruce" first thing the next morning. If you wanna hear "Jingle Bells" come quickly, our tawdry, tasteless, tacky (and toothless!) friend may have a very short shelf life!

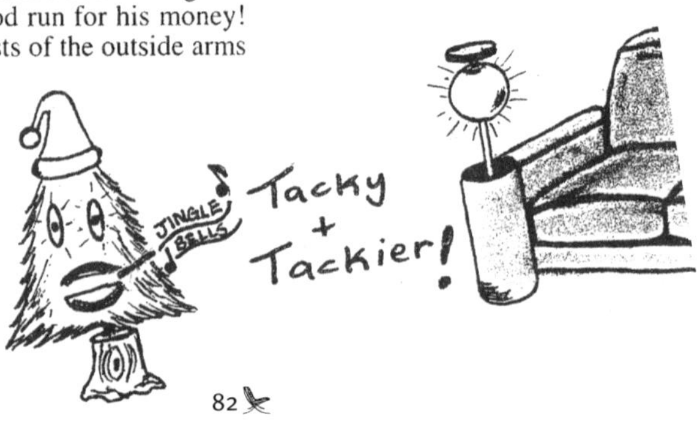

December 13, 1998

Christmas Lights, Snow and Memories

This past Friday was memorable. Besides being the day after my brother's birthday, it snowed.

And it wasn't just a pittance like we've had, it was a bona fide piece of work that's here for the season and I love it!

Now I didn't mind our November that thought it was April, but enough's enough, it's time we stopped planting tulips and Daffodils outside (I planted some on Nov. 22nd!) and took out the toboggans and shovels.

We look on this first "staying" snowfall with dread and trepidation, only to find that it's actually a relief and even fun!

This snowfall was that and more. It clothed the city in an exquisite white coat of virginal beauty that not only bespoke of Christmas piety, but of hope and fellowship, good messages we should carry forward into the next year.

And this pristine cover is an excellent mirror for the dazzling display of lights that bedeck our friendly city.

Because November was so warm, the hanging of Christmas lights was probably done more thoroughly and with more lights. No clambering up ladders this year with an eye to getting back into the house to warm frosty appendages like ears and fingers! You could stay outside longer and actually enjoy the task, as long as you still get to grumble somewhat to let the "distaff" side know how hard you were working!

The lights and snows of Christmas also remind me of my friend Bill.

He always had an outstanding light display at home which he loved to share with his neighbours and his wife Alice, whom he adored.

He owned a gravel company and his huge front-end loaders were contracted out for Winter snow removal.

One magical night he described to me the breathtaking beauty of fresh fallen snow, billowing up in rolling waves before the loader's blades, revealing for a moment the gentle soul behind his sometimes gruff mask.

Bill died last year, but when fresh fallen snow sparkles on the ground, I am blessed with the wonderful memory he shared with me.

December 20, 1998

SMORG OF THE SOUTH!

There were seven buffet bars at the oriental "Smorg" in Fort Lauderdale. The two entree bars alone held eight trays of assorted exotic dishes, per side!

The salad bar must've had eight or ten selections including a huge dish of fresh shrimp, which I generously shared with the general populous.

And did I mention the Sushi bar? I'd say more about the five or six Sushi offerings and the tangy horseradish, fresh peeled ginger and zippy teriyaki sauce but I have a daughter who introduced me to Sushi initially and she's terribly jealous if I go alone. So suffer.

The direct kitchen bar doled out generous portions of prime cut roast beef and other cooked meats, done to perfection.

The dessert bar, as expected, held goodies like key lime pie and exotic puff pastry plus a mixed fruit bowl including fresh citrus items that are grown right there! Huge slices of watermelon and canteloupe also helped deck the bounty!

And then, there was the ice cream bar. My resistance to that wonderful confection is as stiff as the backbone of a slug! And to make it worse there were eight different flavours including scrumptious Pistachio and Almond Mocha that was to die for!

It will forever reside on my conscience that I chose these last two, alas, several times! I told my dear wife that I'm going on a holiday this year. We ain't had one for near ten years and if she wanted to stay in town I would write, or at least drop her an E-mail. She came.

Neither of us can stay away from Winnipeg or Roxy our puppy, for very long so we agreed to go for five days.

We stayed at her sister and brother-in-law's beautiful condo in Fort Lauderdale. Ron was stuck in Winnipeg on business but her sister Sharon, was a most gracious host and we had an absolutely delightful time.

Now I'm not going to say that my wife spent all her time shopping, but the merchants in two of the malls flew their flags at half mast when we left Thursday night!

December 27, 1998

It Came Upon A Summer's Day!

This year I had a different Christmas experience.

It was about a week and a half before Christmas and we were down south for our first holiday in over ten years. There was a fantastic radio station playing a lot of the current "Swing" rage tunes plus a whole raft of music from around that era.

The nostalgia absolutely oozed out of the car radio and we were lapping it up!

The strange part of this experience was that every once in awhile, in keeping with the season, they would play the odd "Winter" type ditty and then a Christmas song.

What a strange feeling that was, hearing someone singing "Baby It's Cold Outside" when you're struggling to keep ahead of the eighty degree Fahrenheit temperature. And then along came the ever beautiful "White Christmas" and there wasn't a glint of snow to be seen anywhere and no hope of any either!

It took me back to a summer long past and one of my fondest Christmas memories ever.

I was in my early teens and riding my bike past some houses that bordered a park in our area. There were a few cardboard boxes laid on the boulevard waiting for a salvage pick up.

I was somehow drawn to a little box. I opened it. It was chock full of cards from many Christmases past. I had never seen so many beautiful things in one little box and with some difficulty, I toted 'em home. I put them under my bed and that night I examined my treasure trove. Even though it was near mid-summer, these beautiful greetings transported me to a wonderful world of pine trees, bells and lights, a lot of smiling faces and of course our glorious white snow!

But the big one was the messages, brimming with good cheer, hope and bountiful wishes of happiness.

Over the years that little box of treasures saw me through some tough times and I still look back with extreme fondness on that summer's day when I found Christmas.

January 3, 1999

PHOO ON THE PHLOO!

If the truth be known, the Florida holiday was superb. It was only a five day sprint (and I mean sprint!), but thanks to by sister-in-law who was indefatigable (that means she don't get tired like her sister!), we got to see lots, eat lots and rested as well as time would allow.

Only one problem. I went there with a minor sore throat but overdoing a few things and trying to crowd a month's holiday into five days, helped it grow into a major problem.

When we were away the weather here was beautiful. (of course we checked every day!) But the evening we returned was when it had snowed all day and then got cold. I didn't bring it back with me, honest!

Well it's been two weeks now and aside for a few short cameo appearances I haven't been outside.

And now there's a real problem. There is absolutely no sympathy in this town for anybody with the flu!

I've just come from lunch across the street at the Lombard. After being a prisoner for two weeks I couldn't wait to go forth, greet the world and receive my well deserved solace from my fellow man.

Yuck, don't come near me with that Flu! This was the well deserved solace I received and worse yet.

"Why don't you stay home when you're sick, 'stead of coughin' and sputterin' and blowin' your nose all 'round here?" This sentence ended with a nickname that described a part of the anatomy I'd rather not mention at this (or any other!)time. I thought at least if I stayed behind my desk I could "ambush" a few customers into listening to my travails. But no, these selfish people rushed in and beat me to the punch! They described their petty little illnesses while giving me hardly a moment to tell them of "MY" great suffering.

I beseeched my wife to make some hot broth for my flu. She said "When did Campbell's go out of business?"

February 7, 1999

CARING, CREATIVE CRATING!

About twenty years ago, we shipped a chest up north by a national carrier. It arrived as ready-made toothpicks! It didn't reach there just somewhat damaged, that can be mended, it had been annihilated!

We thought it had been packaged well and covered with enough 'fragile' labels to get it safely to Rangoon, or at least its destination. The carton had been examined at pick-up and if you've ever gone through the process you know that if it ain't packed properly, the pick-up guys write out a list of exceptions on the shipping bill that completely clears the carrier of all responsibility should it arrive in a damaged condition. (Not our fault, it's the packing!)

Whoever thought truckers are just dense 'lugs' has not experienced the virtuoso performance given when they are writing out exceptions on the shipping bill. A pin hole is listed as a "gouge". A little dirt on the carton becomes evidence of 'severe rubbing'. The list goes on and even gets better but I think you get my drift.

Anyway, the customer put in a claim for the entire cost of the desk, there being nothing salvageable and thought the claim would be settled quickly.

After a long wait, the claim was unbelievably declined. No matter how we argued and filed the necessary documents, it was declined.

I immediately looked into changes that would get an article to its destination even if they rolled it all the way there!

We now create with two by fours and our customers are absolutely amazed at the excellent condition in which our goods arrive.

I told my better half (if I'm such a good guy, why is she called the better half) that we should ship something far away and record its arrival condition to show our customers how well we pack stuff.

'Bout a week later I heard her say to someone on the phone; "Yeah, 'round six feet tall and 175 pounds; dead weight."

"Great idea 'bout something far away" she said, "we're gonna do it".

"Those were my measurements" I said nervously.

"Yep" she said.

February 14, 1999

THIS IS A HOLIDAY?

Know what a busman's holiday is? That's when a guy or gal goes on a holiday and repeats what they do at home. For instance, a travelling salesman who drives all over the place as part of his job, drives all over the place when he takes a holiday. He rarely travels in his business with his family, so for them driving all over is even fun. But I think on vacation, this guy wouldn't mind a bit of a break from the wheel.

Well, we used to take a sort of busman's holiday. When we visited other cities, we would visit as many furniture stores as time allowed.

Actually, a lot of it was job related. When we attended furniture meetings in another city, part of the visit would usually entail a trip to a local furniture store who was doing an outstanding job for the manufacturer who hosted the meeting.

After, we might break up into smaller groups and go "bumming" around town. A lot of times we'd simply go to other stores and see what's doin'.

Because we were from Canada and the meetings were always held in the US, the merchants didn't mind talkin' to us and sharing some of their strategies. At times it was quite enjoyable meeting new and successful people in your industry.

However, these meetings were held in some pretty nice resorts and if I had my druthers, I would've spent a lot more time seeing other things than furniture stores. But I travel with a tough taskmaster and she dragged me into a lot more stores than I wanted to see. Sometimes though, incessant whining would pay off and we'd break away to fun places like Pikes' Peak. What a marvelous time that was! I ran around up there so much that if it wasn't for her I'd have missed the train goin' back down.

That was about 20 years ago, but whenever she recalls the incident she just shakes her head and says: "Why? Why?"

Beats me what she's thinking about.

April 11, 1999

IRA'S DARING DOWNTOWN DELI!

We have an outstanding deli in our lower level. About three and a half years ago we heard that a super deli in the "Nord" end was looking to move downtown.

We had some free space in our lower level and "pitched" it to the deli owners. They seemed willing to take a chance on our "spot" if we could show them a feasible layout.

We have rented out a lot of space over the years, the inexpensive rent making it an ideal storage facility for many downtown offices and retail outlets but we ain't never done a restaurant layout!

So "Les Femmes", my wife and my top designer went to work to design an attractive and practical venue from "raw" space. However, in my naiveté, I did not realize and was not informed that this adventure would entail the two of them traipsing in and out of some of Winnipeg's finest eating spots.

Of course you can't just walk in and look the place over and walk out right away, you've got to bide a while and dine, the food of choice being rich desserts. A more moderate cuisine would have been just fine, but "Les Femmes" insisted on doing it in style to "... get the right ambiance."

Some might say that during this time of personal sacrifice they became somewhat "broad of beam" but there is little truth to this heresy!

The layout was a smashing success and Ira's Deli has been well received in the area. We even gave him a roomy kitchen to facilitate his large catering business.

This week I got a real "lift" when I spotted Ira's Deli among the 1998 Food Service Merit Award winners, no small achievement this award.

Atta boy son. Yep, Ira's our son and his lovely wife Susan our daughter-in-law. And now, more than three years later, you can still find a little old lady at a forward table, telling all who would listen how hard it was to make a deli downstairs.

She might even buy you a bowl of Ira's wonderful soup!

May 9, 1999

THANK YOU JOHNNIE!!!

I know none of you parents have ever said it. However, some children think they may have heard some parents say to their wee bairns: "I hope your children are as bad as you are and you'll see what I've gone through!"

Actually it's the Mother that utters this woeful lament, Father, usually ignores the travail. Although a male scion being scolded may bring a slight smile to his face as his wife's admonition kindles long forgotten memories of youth.

Many of you don't realize that my son Ira, who runs the fabulous deli below us and who is considered kind, sweet and good to animals was an "enfant terrible" in his youth causing even his father to utter a similar reproach.

But then this past winter, the unbelievable happened.

I was sitting alone in Ira's Deli after hours when the phone rang.

"Mr. Brick?" a voice asked. A chill coursed through my body! That voice! Could I ever forget it? It was Ira's teacher from 20 years past and many a time I was on the receiving end of this voice while Ira's behaviour or, lack of it, was spelled out to me in brutal detail.

I knew what was coming and I couldn't believe fate had rewarded me so richly. She wanted to talk to Ira to complain about my grandson's behaviour.

I shamefully answered: "speaking" and it began: "Your son Jonathon and his friends were throwing snowballs at the girls today!" I urged her to tell me more and then more but Jonathon's misdeeds paled before those of his miscreant father and besides, I had drunk enough of the heady elixir.

I ran upstairs and told my wife what had transpired. Shamelessly, a gleeful grin spread over her face.

When Ira returned I donned my most serious countenance and told him of Jonathon's frightful behaviour. But I finally burst out laughing cutting short his torture.

Besides, I never really wanted to do this to him, my wife made me do it. Honest!

May 16, 1999

A BEAUTIFUL SUMMER'S/WINTER'S DAY!

This year May 11th fell on a Tuesday. Twenty years ago it was on a Friday and I awoke that morning to find Winnipeg blanketed by one last snowfall.

It was absolutely gorgeous! And better yet, it wasn't that cold.

When I walked outside to "taste" the fresh, clean air, I found the snow sticking to my shoes.

I quickly ran back into the house and roused my three sons. In our house, rousing my girls was akin to trying to remove a wild bear from a beehive loaded with honey, by reasoning with him, good luck!

Anyway, back to the boys. They didn't know what hit 'em but fairly soon the four of us were in the front yard making a snowman! Mother came to the door to see what was goin' on and quickly shouted to the boys to get ready for school and me for work.

We nodded but there was toiling to be done! We made the base, then struggled to lift the "torso" atop it.

After the head was seated properly the two older boys, unable to withstand the invectives, sadly went off to school.

I remained alone with my youngest, trying vainly to find, in this modern era, two lumps of coal for the eyes and wondering how I could get past my wife to snitch a carrot from the fridge for the nose. But alas, work beckoned me also and I had to leave a mere child to finish this arduous labour. Unfortunately, when my wife came to work later, the grumbling came with her. It subsided suddenly however when she phoned home and learned that a Winnipeg Free Press photographer had appeared and taken a few shots of our melting creation. She couldn't sleep that night and by four in the morning I was forced to drive her down to the paper. We had made page two and I was a hero!

She vainly tried to buy up the entire first run but had to settle for 20 papers.

How do you wallpaper a house with only 20 papers?

April
Showers
bring
May
Flowers
SNOW!

May 23, 1999

THE PEANUT BUTTER CAPERS!

There's an absolutely wonderful little shop in our city that sells foods like we used to have when I was a kid. They're now called organically grown foods, implying that they're grown without pesticides, herbicides, fertilizers or any other of the "good" things they put into the ground or spray on your plant (read: food) to make it grow better (?). When I was a kid we never heard of the words "organically grown", we just popped seeds into the ground and voila, up sprouted our vegetables and flowers.

And I guess I'm not a good 20th century chap cause I prefer the old way we used to grow things. As a matter of fact, a lot of the current food additives make me downright ill!

The reason for this diatribe is so that you should know how strong I feel about getting hold of a jar or container of "pure" peanut butter and how scarce it is in this town! I used to buy it at a large supermarket chain. They carried two different brands along with one of their own.

However the predictable has happened and nowadays they only stock their own brand. I believe it's supposed to be pure but I'm a bit leery cause I think it's homogenized, that is, one consistency, sort of like molasses which does not allow the oil to separate and rise to the top so you can pour it out. I don't like eating too much oil with my peanut butter!

Meanwhile, back at the shop where I discovered "organic" peanut butter. It's also a bit "soupy" but not nearly as oily.

The trouble?

They're almost always sold out!!!

If I had a product that disappeared the same day it was brought in, I'd bring in more product.

There might be a legitimate supply problem but no one's told me about it.

Meantime, my wife, who is hooked on this stuff, thinks I buy some and hide it.

But I got principles, the only thing I hide from her is the TV remote!

Au Naturale!
'Nuttin But Peanuts

June 6, 1999

THE CANDY CAPER!

Remember when you went to restaurants awhile back? They had a bowl of unwrapped candy by the cash which you could help yourself to while paying.

Then news came out that this was very unsanitary. Studies were done and a number of sinister looking germs were found lurking within the bowl.

Nowadays the server brings you a couple of wrapped mints with your tab.

Actually the hotel across the street from us, The Lombard, hands out a couple of butterscotch-like candies wrapped in gold foil every time you receive a bill. I put them in my pocket and when I empty my pants at night I throw them into a candy jar where they accumulate.

And therein lies a ghastly tale! If you can handle it - stay with me!

Last Halloween started out like many others. My wife said: "I'll take the front door, you get the back and don't you dare fall asleep again!"

I'd purchased enough candy to keep 5 dentists in annuities for life but fate was working against me. A new neighbour had recently arrived, and last year, had the most marvelous Halloween display for miles around. (Christmas was even better!)

The news had quickly spread and this year the area was flooded with sightseers.

After this joyful pastime, their kids went collecting treats in the area. The unthinkable happened, we began running out of candy. We panicked till I suddenly thought of the classy looking candy from The Lombard. I got 'em and saved the day (or night!) or so I thought.

My Mother-in-law suddenly became ill and we had to rush down to meet her at emergency.

A couple of my own "kids" had shown up and we told them to man the fort.

When we returned we were met at the door with: "How tacky! Giving out candy from The Lombard! We'll be ruined!"

"But the crowds, the crowds ..." we tried to explain. We were cut off in mid-sentence while the "kids" left in a haughty poise, bums protruding and noses in the air!

HOTEL
CANDY
IS VERY
HANDY!
(AND DANDY!)

July 18, 1999

"IT AIN'T OVER TILL IT'S OVER"

This is a terrible time of year for me. It's too early to put away your garden tools and too late and too hot to do much more productive planting.

You can always do clean up chores, weeding and hoeing, but for meatier, "where's the beef?" kind of gardening you gotta wait till the leaves start dropping. Of course I could go back to my roots (pun intended!) and start putting in more time at the furniture store, but after the frenzied garden season just past, how do you get back to a normal routine?

I've never seen a garden season quite like this one. No matter where you went, from full blown garden nurseries like T & T Seeds, Shelmerdine's, Arbo's and so many others, the places were jam packed! I've seen crowds at the beginning of the season but line-ups in late June? Gimme a break!

And to make matters, one chap laid about eight Dahlia rhizomes on me. I haven't planted Dahlias for years.

Paddy Twomey introduced me to Dahlias years ago and for about fifteen years or so I had some beautiful shows.

Then, the place where I would normally plant them became infested with tree roots and I ain't "done Dahlias" for years. Now with eight bursting rhizomes and a severely short time left to get blooms, what'll I do?

To make matters worse, I promised the wife I'd get off my butt and get our fall sales organized.

And to make matters really tough I just leased a beautiful new car. It's sorta red with a black top that's kinda like cloth which has a habit of folding up. Sorta, kinda a convertible.

Mid-life crisis? You betcha!

So if you see a white-haired guy with sunglasses and a dog half out of a red convertible and both have big grins, it's me and Roxy.

If I'm flying past a certain furniture store on Lombard and a woman is standing at the door shaking her fists, tell her I'll be back at work, sorta, kinda soon!

August 1, 1999

PAN AM WINNIPEG - HOT, COLD AND WONDERFUL!

Have we got heat! It's hard to believe that in a few short months the shorts we're now wearing will be just a memory. The ground will likely have had at least a dusting of our white and fluffy (and freezing and slippery!) mantle, commonly called snow by visitors. As our winter drags on, us regulars give it other, "flavourful" names.

If we're really clever we'll make friends with some of our warmer climate visitors in town for the Pan Am games and arrange to visit them when the winds of change make our thermometers register thirty degrees at the reverse end of the scale, below zero!

Actually some of us look forward to our winter season, these lazy, hazy (and hot!) days of summer sap the drive out of some of us and we seem to function better in the cool (!), brisk days of winter.

This may be a hard thing to remember when you've just slid into a snowbank, it's twenty or thirty below zero, shovelling seems hopeless and dynamite is illegal!

It might also be hard to remember when there's a power failure at thirty below or worse and your furnace goes south for the winter.

The media is warning you to turn off all unnecessary applicances and lights and you sit shivering in the dark wondering why your parents chose a northern clime and didn't even give you a vote!

But while we ain't got baseball we got hockey.

We ain't got outdoor track and field but we got skiing and curling. In fact we got some of the best curlers in the world!

We got "Le Festival du Voyageur", one of the country's best French fêtes including a wonderful dash of culture, cuisine, affection and absolutely awesome ice sculptures!

C'est bon!

We can swim and play some pretty demanding physical games indoors and more better yet, there's no mosquitoes!!! You know, maybe some of our wonderful guests might wanna come here for a taste of real livin'. And you know what? We'd love to have 'em!

August 8, 1999

FROM CAVEMAN TO BEACH BOY!

Remember the Piltdown man? In the early 1900's parts of a skull and jawbone were located in a gravel pit in Sussex, England. For years the remains were touted as a "missing link" between man and the Apes.

To settle a developing controversy the remains were tested. The jaw was found to be from a modern ape and the skull from a man about 1250 BC. Some missing link! The Piltdown man was bogus, a fake, a sham, a hoax! The mavens who authenticated this wondrous discovery found themselves looking quite gullible, to say the least.

Of more recent vintage, I recall the career of one Tiny Tim, an entertainer who gained fame plunking a ukulele and singing in a falsetto or some such high-pitched voice. I always believed this started out as a hoax that actually caught on and launched Tiny Tim on a brief career that was too successful to stop! He even got married on the "Tonight" show! His rendition of "Tiptoe Through The Tulips" was a popular ditty at the time.

And where does this lead us?

Where else but to "Beach Volleyball", perhaps the bestest hoax of our time! I believe mischievous people, taking advantage of the acute susceptibility of older men to criticism from any quarter that shouts "Sexist" at them, presented this "Sport" to said older men as deserving of Olympic status.

When Beach Volleyball was played at the Olympics in Atlanta, I thought it was a bit of fun that would die quickly, as did most of the guys and gals I talked to. Though the scant outfits of the female participants gave rise to a great concern lest they become chilled and were taken ill. I'm sure it was this concern that had most TV sets in the world tuned in to watch this "Sport".

Now that the Pan Am games have ended in our fair city, I think this Hoax will be shortly exposed (no pun intended) and Sydney, whoever he is, won't have to put up with this shtick next year!

August 15, 1999

WASN'T THAT A PARTY!

The second week in August has always been a memorable one for me, at least for the past 20 years or so.

It's the week that two of my sons have birthdays and brings back a memorable week in Montreal about 23 years ago.

It all started with Denis, a buddy of mine. Him and his wife would motor down from Toronto and meet us in Montreal while attending a Canadian Furniture Market. His wife, who loved quality furniture, would attend the show with us and Denny would tear around Montreal with our three delinquents.

In the evenings we dined out. The second evening we were at Dunn's delicatessen. Their window displayed a marvellous assortment of pickles, smoked meats and other exotic food stuffs! Yummy! They had a live band and a top female vocalist.

Suddenly the lights dimmed, the singer came down from the stage, walked to our table and with band playing, belted out Happy Birthday! It was my son Robbie's birthday and he could barely talk, a temporary loss for which he has since made up for in spades!

Two days later it was my other son Ira's birthday. We were heading back and still had no plans for his birthday. While boarding, I told the stewardess my problem. She said: "Point him out and leave it to me."

It was a supper flight just before sunset. After dinner the stewardess approached our seats.

Looking straight at this teenage ruffian she said: "Mr. Ira Brick?"

"Uh yeah, uh, yeah," he muttered in perfect broken English and gazed towards me. Before anyone could comment she continued: "The captain was wondering if you would like to spend some time with him, in the cockpit."

This time speech wouldn't come, he just nodded and followed her to the front. We never saw him the rest of the flight. The sun was setting in all its splendour and they, him and the crew, "chased" it all the way back to Winnipeg.

Ring up one more fantastic birthday.

Thanks Denis and thanks Air Canada!

August 29, 1999

WILLPOWER AND THE DEMON WEED!

It may be hard for some of you to believe that an outstanding and righteous soul such as I could ever have indulged in what some people consider an obnoxious habit. "What'd he do?" I can hear you asking yourselves in disbelief, some even wringing their hands in shock!

In a word, or two, I tasted the demon Devil's wicked Weed; terrible Tobacco! I smoked and "went-all-the-way", I inhaled. And, if the truth be known, I liked it! I'd deeply suck in this elixir, then exhale and watch the wisps casually curl upward.

However, there were a tad few drawbacks. For instance, I suffer from Bronchitis and when I caught a cold, which was often, breathing was so laborious I could frighten even bratty children into doing their homework!

Worse yet, I had a spouse who didn't catch colds and who would measurably increase my misery by screeching out admonitions such as: "If I suffered like you do (I wish!) with your colds, I'd quit smoking!"

My reply, though dazzling and exuding brilliant wit is somewhat, or even lotswhat, unprintable. And then it happened. The gods, tired of her biting critiques to a wonderful but suffering mate, did cause her to be smitten with a lusty chest cold.

Being so wonderful I did not rejoice. I waited instead for her to recover so I could "gently" tease her about her inability to quit her two-pack a day habit.

But I was faced with a horrid consequence, she quit. She never smoked again!

This woman, who could do nothing, and I mean nothing, without a cigarette in her "mitt or mouth", reached down deep into her entrails, found "Willpower" and quit smoking!

In a brazen display of this same fiery brand of "Willpower" I put her to shame by quitting shortly after even though I had smoked more heavily and for a much longer time!

Some skeptics say 5 years is not shortly after.

I pity them. They are merely jealous of my firm resolve.

September 19, 1999

THE LITTLE SHOWER THAT WASN'T!

Sometime in May this year, my wife decided we needed a shower in the downstairs "Executive" washroom. She already hides the water cooler there so it was only a minor step for her to ensconce a shower in the same site.

I informed her that a locale was already available in one of the upstairs washrooms that had previously contained a shower. It made little sense to use up prime office space when everything, including privacy, was almost in readiness upstairs.

She agreed.

'Bout a week later when I came into the office after a series of morning appointments, I was shocked to find workmen preparing space for a shower stall behind the main office.

"What on Earth ..." I sputtered.

"Oh, it'll be for you too. Remember how you always want a shower here after you come downtown by bike?"

"But on the second floor, the second floor ...", my voice fell on deaf ears as she kept on with more inane reasons for a main floor, prime space, shower stall.

As usual I let her have her way and perhaps if space was sorely needed, we could just set up a desk in the shower stall, perhaps even when it's not being used!

Two days later when I waltzed in, (I do have a flair), I found, to my consternation, instead of an inexpensive little stall, it had glass doors and lots of chrome trim. The interior was molded and sleek with shelves for everything!

"How much?" I gently asked. "You'll love it." she said.

"How Much?" I asked again.

"Wait'll you see it all finished." she said.

"When?" I asked.

"In a few days." she said.

It is now mid-September. Drywall dust is all over the place, the rear office is piled high with stuff and we're nowhere near finished!

In the meantime the plumber and electrician are planning exotic cruises and I'm getting more than somewhat overheated.

Course, I can always take a cold shower!

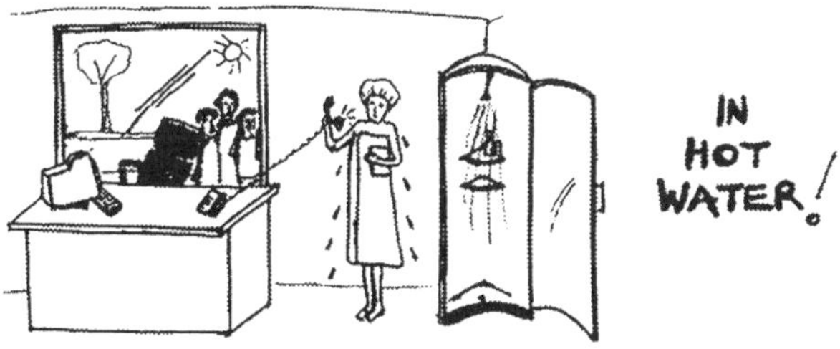

September 26, 1999

BANGS, BONGS AND BOOGY MEN!

When we were just starting out in the furniture business things were pretty tight. We didn't have a whole lot of money so when a furniture salesman who called on us at that time asked us if we could store his other line of merchandise I said "yes". It was furniture in a way, wooden, had upholstery and you could lay down in it. That's in it, not on it! He sold coffins. My wife shot me a chagrined glare in spite of which we went into the casket storage business. They were crated and we stashed them on our third floor behind closed doors. If anybody perchance spotted the crates, we said they were triple dressers!

We stay open Friday nights then as we do now, but back then they were long, lonely nights waiting for customers.

This particular night was quieter than most. We were just chatting on a sofa when suddenly from the upper floor came a resounding crash. We looked at one another, wild thoughts going through our minds, but said nothing.

We sat there in stony silence, hardly breathing, when another crash echoed through our showroom.

After two more I said: "I've gotta look upstairs".

She said: "I'm coming too, I'm too scared to stay downstairs alone."

As we slowly crept up the stairs another boom rang out, but we continued, albeit with failing hearts!

At the top of the stairs, as I opened the door to the coffin room a tremendous pair of crashes burst forth.

We ran down the stairs, grabbed our car keys and took off. To the 'Cop Shop'. They were gracious. They tried hard not to laugh when we told the story and agreed to follow us back.

As we came down our street we spotted some activity in the empty lot before our building. Our 'GHOSTS' turned out to be a bunch of kids throwing rocks at the windows of our building.

The cops were polite but couldn't stop laughing.

"How'dja feel?" I asked my wife.

"Sheepish" she said, sort of 'Eweish'.

"Funny, I said, you don't look it!"

October 17, 1999

CORNSTALKS AND BALES OF HAY! (AND A RED CONVERTIBLE!!)

We haven't got a name for him yet but he's sorta adorable, a mite scary and a whole lot of fun.

He's quite tall and surrounded by cornstalks, bales of hay, pumpkins and a lot of good cheer.

He sits outside our front door and is unflappable, giving his placid (but cute!) grin to all who walk by.

Whoozzit? Or whatzzit?

Why he's our genuine homemade Scarecrow!

We were all sitting around last week, even my wife (who works 60 hours a week while "HE" runs around in that convertible!) when Linda said: "Why don't we make a scarecrow for the front door?"

"I love it" I said, "What'll we need?"

"Firstly we'll need some hay, without the sowbug population that you got last time."

"Done" I said, "I'll call Ernie at Saddock Nursery and if he ain't got any he'll know where to go."

"No, no" said my wife, "It'll get all messy in here."

"Then we'll need a shirt and pants and a whole lot of things" continued Linda paying no mind to the no no's.

And so, like the good Dr. Frankenstein of monster fame, we built a creature, not a living, breathing one but a gentle creature, a sort of "Frosty the Snowman" kinda guy. Susan brought a Red plaid shirt and Linda got a straw hat.

A pair of jeans was contributed by Lisa and Cindy from downstairs gave us fabric for his head.

Cornstalks were gotten from an unknown garden and long johns were another mysterious "gift" that just somehow appeared.

And finally, it was all assembled at night by the "gifted artiste" Raymond, who works during the day as one of our shipper receivers. (Raymond don't give up your day job!)

The other two guys at the back, Mike and Stuart, donated us their labour (and mutterings!) by hauling our illustrious scarecrow and his "retinue" in and out every day.

What'd I do? Not much. You see I spend all day running around in a little red convertible!

A NOT SO SCARY STORY.... sort of

October 31, 1999

PAVING STONES, LAMPPOSTS AND CHIRPING BIRDS!

Big things are happening. Well, maybe not so big, but nice.

For instance as I've said before we got a scarecrow outside our front door and he ain't going anywhere till after Halloween!

And then, just before the Pan Am Games the city came down with a crew and they redid the pavement in front of our shop.

Now they really didn't redo the pavement they removed it(!) and replaced it with those sexy paving stones and it really turned out great!

More better yet, they planted two lovely ash trees amongst the paving stones and topped the whole thing off with a pair of dramatic, period lampposts. You wanna talk gorgeous? This is gorgeous!

And Lombard Avenue used to continue for a very short block past our building but now instead of stopping at the end, just before that awesome railroad bridge, it gently curves past the bridge and meanders behind our magnificent new baseball stadium, (Thanks Sam!) and connects up with the roads leading onto and away from the Provencher Street bridge.

Once again, gorgeous!

And now that we got a pair of little trees outside our windows, guess what Linda did? She located a little bird feeder somewhere in the trees.

Then of course I had to truck on down to Victor Fox Foods on James Avenue almost directly behind Athletes Wear and bought a 50 pound bag of Wild Bird Seed for close to what you'd probably pay for a 15 or 20 pound bag at the supermarkets.

This is wonderful for the girls 'cause instead of gossiping and reading the newspaper all day they can now look out the window and watch the birdies!

I gave Susan some seed to take to her apartment but she said I gave her too much 'cause the birds will chirp so much in the morning, they'll wake her up too early.

"Good", I told her, "then maybe you'll get to work on time!"

November 14, 1999

REMEMBRANCE

I remember fresh fallen snow sparkling like gems on the ground.

And I remember sticking my tongue out and catching them as they fell.

I remember playing on the kitchen floor near my Mom while she was ironing.

And her shrieks of delight, when our apartment door opened to reveal my brother in uniform, home on leave.

I remember the night when he came home when the war was over. He rubbed my head so hard it hurt, but it felt good.

I remember going with my Dad to buy fresh fruit and vegetables at the "Fruit Row" on Ross Avenue, the shouting, the hustle and the odours were magic to a young boy's senses.

I remember those clanging streetcars and the best seats in winter, those near the firebox.

I remember the magic of the first fluorescent lights I ever saw at the Prague cafe on Main Street.

I remember my two most favourite songs, "Somewhere over the Rainbow" by Judy Garland and "The White Cliffs of Dover" by Vera Lynn.

I remember unlocking the street sewers in the springtime as a kid, what wonderful fun.

I remember riding my bike to a field at the city limits and catching toads and lettin' 'em go.

I remember lyin' on the grass in summer and looking up at the clouds,

And my dog Bowser, ever beside me who would torment the cats on our street.

I remember the French radio station coming on the air with a beautiful diet of classical music, and "Porky" Charbonneau of old CKY radio with an equally good fare of western strains.

I remember the trolley bus overhead wires being rolled up, never to grace our streets again.

I remember my Uncle Mac visiting from West Virginia and his lovely family, especially Mimi who I adored.

But most of all I remember all those family friends who never came home from the war, so that we may enjoy our memories and live to make more.

Bless them all, Bless them all, the young the short and the tall ...

November 28, 1999

IT'S A DOG'S LIFE!

Work in the office of Brick's Fine Furniture Ltd. has come to a screeching halt!

"Les femmes," Linda and Susan are petting "ma chère amie" Roxy, who is lying on the office floor on her back! Maybe I should also tell you that Roxy is a dog, a medium, little-sized Terrier-Miniature-Pincher cross who captures everybody's heart.

Like me, to know her is to love her!

She is the consummate petting animal. I have had many dogs in my life and they all wanted to be stroked but this one's somethin' else!

She'll approach perfect strangers, especially women, and spots something in their psyche immediately 'cause she stands up, puts her two front paws on them and invariably gets stroked. It's uncanny how she can select those who not only tolerate animals but who like dogs and will pet her.

And once you start, this animal is insatiable. If you stop petting her, she pushes her snout under your arm or hand until you resume. If you don't, she starts to "talk". She mutters, whines and growls and starts folding her body in a semi-circle. Very few can put up with this performance without relenting and starting the petting and stroking process again and again.

When Susan began here a couple of years ago she didn't know that from time to time a dog would become part of her working life.

The first time she saw Roxy she shied away. She had grown up with a fear of dogs, having been bitten in her formative years. To make it a little scarier, Roxy was very excited to meet the new "kid on the block".

Now, when I come in without Roxy, I get a look from Susan that's enough to give me a complex.

Here I walk in, the symbol of joy and good fortune and I get this look of dismay because Roxy ain't with me!

I think I'll go buy a pair of floppy ears and a stick-on wet nose and see if I can at least get a grin!

December 26, 1999

CAN A DOG BE A HAM?!

Can you believe that when we were having our 32 below zero day this past Monday it was 2 above in Calgary and six above in Vancouver?

Heck, on December 2nd the girls took a picture of me in shorts! A chap came in during our "Big Chill" and of course we talked about the weather. He said something like:"We got lulled into thinking we were tough and were just enjoying the warm weather!"

Boy did he hit it right on the nose! We were getting well used to the unseasonable warmth when the cold descended upon us and we got un-tough very quickly! Brrrr!

But it got warm just in time for Christmas and the holiday has brought my son Robert, his wife Krista, and Aliya, my third grandchild, home for the holidays.

Aliyah can now say Mummy and Daddy with a degree of clarity and "NO" with a lot of oomph! And I'll probably get to see the other two grandchildren more. I pick Paula up from her daycare once in a while and I look forward to spend some time with Jonathon.

I used to love going out and shovelling my driveway and walk over the holidays. I really enjoy shovelling and thought I had impressed that mightily on my wife. So, 'bout four years ago, she buys me a snowblower! Go figure!

And the holiday season has brought a bounty, not for me, but for my dog Roxy. Susan, fully supported by her mentor Linda, bought Roxy a sweater. It's a blue and red stripe and she looks like a convict!

The girls put it on her and I think she wondered if it'll hamper her when she's chasing squirrels!

That was Wednesday. On Thursday we had a photo-op. They dressed Roxy up in her expensive, yes expensive, outer garment and shamelessly took photo after photo of our new fashion plate, Roxy!

I told them she was embarrassed but if the truth be known, I think Roxy's a real ham!

AGENT K-9
(AKA ROXY)
IN"DOG"NITO!

February 13, 2000

CALL OF THE WILD!

Have you ever hung up on somebody phoning you without even talking to them?

Well I do it on both my new portable cell phone and my new cordless one at home and I might add, it ain't my fault!

My old cordless had a range of about ten feet from its base station. If I went upstairs it was useless. Going out in the yard and taking the phone was a standing joke!

But it wasn't till my mother-in-law needed a new cordless one that I finally broke down and got one for myself as well.

My cell phone, a supposed digital wonder, was not putting through a large percentage of my calls. I would miss appointments, dates with questionable women, racing results and other good stuff.

So a couple of weeks later I changed my cell phone also, thereby unknowingly inviting some sort of satanic evil into my life.

You see the "ON" and "OFF" buttons on both phones are in opposite places. As I use both quite extensively this has led to a nightmare of confusion.

When either phone rings, I have a 50% chance of either answering the caller or hanging up on them!

On really good days, those when I try to concentrate hard on making the right move, I can miss up to 100% of my calls!

You would think the electronics industry would have some degree of standardization but as long as Macy's ain't gonna talk to Sanyo! And it really gets bad in the car where I'm busy trying to remember that the window controls on my new GM car are opposite to the ones of my old GM car!

So when the phone rings and I miss the call and mutter some cute phrase that can peel wallpaper, only to hear a voice on the other end say: "Hello, hello, is that you Fred?"

I disguise my voice, mutter: "No!" and quickly hang up while Roxy, that supposedly cute dog of mine, rolls around laughing in the back seat!

February 20, 2000

A TOUCH OF SPRING!

What have primroses and begonias got in common? Or for that matter, what do Kalanchoes and miniature Roses share together?

Well, they're all beautiful flowering plants and they're doin' it right now! A lot of the big box and not so big box stores are selling 'em in little two, three or four inch pots (and even some larger ones!). They're blooming profusely and even better, they don't cost a heck of a lot!

For years and years, Linda, our head designer, has dashed into the office, rarely on time, in mid-February with rosy red cheeks, bursting with the news that: "Primroses are in bloom at Safeway or Wal-Mart or wherever!"

This year however it happened to be miniature roses.

I curse myself 'cause my secret desire has been, for just one year to be able to also burst into the office in mid-February, also late as usual and exclaim: "The Begonias are blooming, the Begonias are blooming!" but I can never remember to do that. Rats!

This is not just an informative message she brings, the not so hidden meaning is: Get your butt outta here and buy some of these little beauties for the shop!

What she does when they arrive, besides feigning surprise, is arrange them in a large basket, bowl or other container, so that they resemble a bouquet of flowers. They look gorgeous! The pots are hidden under a topping of sphagnum moss and since they are potted, they keep for quite a long time!

All you gotta do is make sure they're properly watered, not too much please(!), and given a bit of light occasionally.

We have some bouquets in areas where there's very little light, so from time to time we'll move them into the light as an invigorating refresher before they "go back to work!"

Everybody loves 'em except our spoiled dog, Roxy. Last time I brought flowers to work and "Les Femmes" fussed over them and ignored her, she was royally teed off!

Fame is so fleeting.

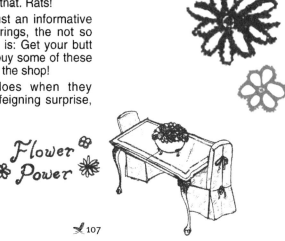

June 18, 2000

GENERAL HOSPITAL, SORT OF!

"Undress," she said.

"Why?" I said.

"Undress," she repeated.

"I don't wanna," I said, "Besides I'm not hurt and I wanna see how my wife is.

"Your wife's fine. Now just undress," she insisted.

"But," I also insisted, "If I'm not hurt why should I undress?"

" 'Cause," she said, "The process of undressing demands a lot of movements that can expose unseen or unfelt injury."

"You know Doc" I said to her. "What a great line! Thank you!" and began disrobing.

No, this ain't no romance novel, it's actually a true story that began with my wife and I going to do volunteer work for a friend of ours, Dr. Sheila Cantor.

The work consisted of being hosts at a charity Bingo being run for the Schizophrenia Society which Sheila headed at that time.

We'd done this before, selling Bingo cards and tending to other chores on these game nights, even after putting in a full day at our jobs.

But Sheila was so dedicated with the work she was doing that her enthusiasm engulfed you and no matter how tired you were, you attended and worked in a smoky room till late and, tired as she was, Sheila worked right alongside us!

But this night we didn't make it. I was driving to the game site, a large building on McPhillips Street about 6:00 p.m. when a tank, carefully disguised as an old Chevy, went blissfully through a red light and *creamed* us on the passenger side in our little Hyundai!

We ended up atop the fire hydrant on the corner.

I was able to get out but it took the "Jaws of Life" some forty minutes or so to free Cynthia from her perch atop the hydrant!

We were both taken to Health Sciences Centre for examination. My wife ended up with several more bruises. She bruises so easy she just has to sneeze!

I escaped with no injuries and a great line, which I was never able to use and a great story, which I just did!

July 9, 2000

THESE MOOSE DON'T PLAY NO HOCKEY!!!!

I was in Toronto this past week and much as I hate to admit it, I really like the city. They do fun stuff like for instance they're currently in love with mooses! Really! One night we were in the Yorkdale Mall and my brother said to me in a calm manner: "Look at the moose."

To me, a large live moose trapped in a shopping mall can be a serious threat to life and limb. I became a little perturbed, but what he points to is a life size, or close to it, statue of a big moose complete with antlers and hooves but bedecked in a suit!

My brother tells me that there's some five to six hundred moose in the city at all kinds of different locations from inside malls to outside of many stores, restaurants or wherever.

So the next day when I went back to the mall to visit a certain shop, I couldn't help but notice that near the middle of the mall was a genuine artificial moose part entitled: (what else!?) "YORKDALE MOOSE PARK." Though it wasn't all that large it housed four huge moose. (Would plurals be meeses?) One was titled Tourist Moose and was clad in a large, actually huge, red and black plaid shirt, a Tilley hat, sunglasses, again huge sunglasses, with a camera 'round its neck! The second moose was just a poor relative and only had a shirt, albeit huge.

The third or Bay Street Moose had on a light blue suit, an off-white shirt and a snazzy tie. The fourth one was a Canadian First Nations Moose and wore an exquisite blanket with symbolic decorations.

The Moose Park General store sold a variety of "Kitschy" moose offerings such as key chains, magnets and believe it or not moose droppings!

They also had all kinds of stuffed meeses including one that lolled around all day, (like some people I work with) and one that played O Canada when he was wound up! Roxy my dog says there's one in every family!

"Bruce" the Moose on the Loose!

August 13, 2000

URBAN DELIGHT!

In the heart of the concrete jungle, in the very eye of the business vortex, in the midst of the downtown core, here, surrounded by cars screeching brakes, trucks belching deadly fumes and addicts hanging outside buildings gasping, coughing and puffing that innocuous weed, amidst all this proliferation of urbanity we have an oasis, a four foot by six foot landlocked garden, a veritable Eden just outside our office windows!

Last Fall the city bestowed upon our outdoor patio a pair of ash trees about twenty feet apart.

Our designers complained that the one directly in front of the window they gander out of all day needed a bird feeder which they just happened to find and quickly attached it to the tree.

Carloads, or at least a pail, of birdseed was procured and zipped into the feeder *tout suite* and customers were left to their own devices as *Les Femmes* were preoccupied watching for the arrival of flocks of voracious feathered denizens.

They came. Not in hordes but rather in trickles, at first anyway. And then in increasing numbers until we had a feeding station that was vying with Ira's Deli in our lower level for head count and also taking big bites out of petty cash! Now here's the rub. Anyone who has ever watched birds at a feeding station will know their table manners are akin to teenagers. I'm sure that for every seed ingested they scatter ten on the ground, but it ain't wasted as the guys who don't get privileges at the feeder can munch the stuff that falls to the ground.

However there's a bit of trouble. When the city planted the ash trees, they surrounded the base with a metal grate and the food that falls there is lost, or so we thought!

Voila! It germinated and has given us our urban garden, brimming with tame millet and sunflowers!

This is all well and good, except that to get *Les Femmes*' attention, I have to run outside and stand in front of that silly Ash tree!

April 8, 2001

EVERY DOG HAS ITS DAY, BUT NO HAMBURGER!

I go for a walk in the park most every morning. I try to be there 'bout 7:00 am and sooner of late 'cause the sun's comin' up earlier and ain't that great!

But this past Thursday, I wasn't moving too quickly. I'd done some stretching and stuff at a therapy session the previous day and I thought, like other times, that I'd wake up the next day and be rarin' to go!

No dice! The hare turned into a tortoise, a very tired tortoise! I stayed in bed till 'bout 7:30 and would have stayed there longer if some pesky little four legged critter called Roxy hadn't started agitating for some outdoor time. You see, Roxy accompanies me near every morning on these walks although a lot of people who see how she pulls me along on the leash have a somewhat different idea of who's accompanying who!

Roxy has put on a bit of weight over the past year and a half and with all the walking we do, wasn't showing any signs of losing her larder. Then 'bout a month ago, when she wanted to return to the car after only an hour's walk, I became worried 'bout her.

So I took her to our vet, Seven Oaks Veterinary Hospital. I told him that she's tiring early in our walks and doesn't seem to be shedding any weight.

He asked 'bout her diet. I told him that she gets lots of hamburger 'cause I'd heard that was supposed to be really great for dogs as they are after all, carnivores.

He examined her thoroughly, then quickly removed her from the high protein, high fat diet, gave me some pills to 'tighten' her stomach and a more balanced diet.

Now, after 'bout a month, she's trimmer, sleeker and does five or six miles with ease.

But there's one small problem, she pulls on that darn leash so hard that my arms are getting longer and I've developed an insatiable appetite for bananas!

April 22, 2001

LA CHORALE DES INTREPIDES. WOW!

Just before Christmas last year I attended a choral concert at St.-Eugene Church on St. Mary's Road with two exciting (excited?) Ladies, one of whom is an avid supporter of our Francophone community.

I don't attend choral concerts, the music being too sonorous and moody for me. Wrong! I was completely blown away by the magnificence of the performance!

Well, on Tuesday night I et les femmes willingly attended another choral concert by this same wondrous group, LES INTREPIDES et les petits intrepides, the younger adjuncts!

There was a difference. There were many more voices and not just an accompanying piano but a very capable orchestra.

There was also another difference, a guest appearance by a Manitoba born vocalist Daniel Lavoie. I'd never heard of M. Lavoie but apparently he is well known outside my narrow venue in places like Paris, where he starred for some time in the opera, Notre Dame de Paris! Now I doubt if I will ever forget him! He has a deep, full voice with an overwhelming richness. C'est magnifique!

The first half of the program seemed to be rather ambitious with classical pieces I thought perhaps beyond the competence of a "local" choral society.

Wrong again! The concert master, M. Marcien Ferland seemed equally at home with the more quaint offerings presented at the Christmas concert last year as with Vivaldi and Borodin. The Polovtsian Dance sequence alone left me breathless!

The junior up-and-comers acquitted themselves very well, their numbers being met with noisy applause!

The second half was better yet with the haunting Ukrainian chant, Hospodi pomilui and the ever entertaining solo, If I were a rich man. The French ditty, Je n'avais que 50 cents (I only have 50 cents) was a funny, raucous bit that produced gales of laughter.

All in all it was once again a wonderful night.

Merci à ma chère amie Louise for introducing me to the beautiful people and culture, carefully guarded just over the Provencher bridge.

PS: Louise, this only gets you a coffee, not supper! But we'll talk!

April 29, 2001

WHEN THE WARRANTY GOES SOUTH!

When a car gets older it starts to develop a few flaws and breaks down now and then. We mutter that the car's becoming a 'bucket of bolts' and start looking at newer models.

We don't say it's going into its golden years, its rusty era would be more like it!

But as we get older we soften the blow by calling the future the Golden Years. So, when our "plumbing" and "joints" start giving us trouble we're somewhat shocked. Nobody told us this would happen in our golden years, maybe to others but not us!

Nobody told me that when I reached those golden years, somewhere past 49, that I'd need help getting up when I bent down to pick up something.

They didn't tell me my kids wouldn't listen to my wise advice and would mutter something about a Mr. Alzheimer when I offered same. And nobody told me that I'd never make it downstairs without going back up at least two more times to get stuff I forgot the first time 'cause I keep forgetting what I went back upstairs to get!

And who said your feet would get so cold at night?

And I never thought that I, like my father before me, could fall asleep in a chair, while someone's talking to me!

And who'd guess that the reason I'm kneeling for such a long time in the garden is 'cause I can't get up! And how about when you suddenly realize that the silence you're "hearing" is because you can't! And you don't trim your own toenails 'cause what you call 'near' vision has gone up and gone 'far' away!

And did I complain about the knees without mentioning shoulders, thighs, neck and whatever is supposed to move smoothly but don't anymore?!

And yet there are golden moments like my five 'kids' and five grandchildren, walks in the park and a cool glass of water.

And a red convertible to aggravate everybody and Roxy, my faithful mutt to share it with!

October 21, 2001

THE PRICE OF FREEDOM - USE OR LOSE IT

We flew out near noon this past Wednesday to the furniture show in North Carolina. I have never see our airport so quiet. Terrorism has indeed kept lots of people from flying, giving voice to the silence of fear.

Even though the crowds weren't there, security was! We passed through three maybe four check points before we were allowed upstairs to the departure lounge.

Amusingly, a security officer asked me for photo ID, then quickly looked up at me and said "That's the face I look at every Sunday in my newspaper!"

We changed planes at Chicago's O'HARE airport and once again experienced the new, tougher, security. But we were getting used to standing in line and the mandatory search of our carry-on luggage. I don't think I opened up my attaché case more times in any other morning!

The chilling part however was in our passage from our arrival gate to our departure gate. We passed several soldiers with loaded rifles in fatigues. Our world had indeed changed.

Our hotel in Greensboro is one of the most sought after at Showtime. We were lucky to get rooms even though we booked them back in June.

However, September 11th must have cost the hotel many cancellations as the "crowds" seemed much sparser. The same held true for the shuttle bus taking people to the market. Once at the show, you could tell the same 'cause people fighting to squeeze on the elevator, always a battle, were sizeably down! The gossip at the show was that the decrease in attendance this year was down around thirty to thirty five percent or more.

And yet, those of us there felt we were doing something worthwhile in attending the show and going about our business.

Retailers and manufacturers alike were sending out a message that while we stopped to console and mourn, the horrors past and those that might be facing us, America and the rest of the free world, will NOT kowtow to the pestilence of terrorism!

December 23, 2001

COOKIES, FURNITURE AND DON'T FEED THE DOG

A coupla weeks ago I wrote about our suppliers, feeling the pinch of a general business malaise, were shipping goods scheduled for shipment in the new year, with an immediacy not known in the industry for years!

Newly ordered case goods, you know wooden stuff like bedroom, dining room and occasional tables, which can take up to six months to arrive, arrived *tout suite!*

Our gorgeous accessories were hitting our floor within a week or so of our return from the furniture shows!

And soft goods, stuff like sofas, love seats and chairs were also shipped early but thank goodness, items ordered for further selling were held back, or so we thought! They've also arrived, just as we were getting some breathing room!

So, need a classy Brick's sofa for the holiday season and beyond at super duper prices? We got 'em and we ain't got no room for 'em. So, in a rare move, we'll be selling lots of these new pieces *right off the floor,* instead of just taking orders!

However, I'll still be taking a couple of orders, such as, "you and the mutt keep off the floor 'cause we're busy!" And the all time favorite, "Stop playing on the computer and get us more coffee!"

Further, the aroma of fresh baked cookies has been noticeably absent from our showroom floor. I've heard a variety of excuses like, "We're so busy we're just too tired!" or "The stores are out of the ingredients"! And the Mother of terrible excuses, "Your dog Roxy eats them all!"

This is a slanderous fiction to cover the true reason for our lack of scrumptious delectability!

I thought it was simple laziness, but the plot (and even the batter!) thickens! It seems that certain staff have been devouring with great haste and even speed, said cookies as soon as they hit the showroom, the aroma being utterly unresistable. So, I announce here and now that adequate quantities of scrump-deelee-icious cookies will be in generous supply over the foreseeable future!

P.S. Please don't feed Roxy or we'll have to call her *Waddle!*

May 19, 2002

THIS BALL HAD IT ALL!

Last Saturday, the combination of office and yard work, wearied my brain and back. However, the Policeman's Ball, being held at the Fairmont Hotel beckoned me, as it does every year!

Our seating was located at the periphery, the outside tables, but we were fortunate to sit with people we knew. A good start that soon got better.

The MC's were Murray Parker and Jim Ingebritsen (I sure hope that's the rite speling)! By themselves, these two bums are terrific! As a duo, they're more better!

Their banter is snappy and refreshing! (Has anybody ever called you guys refreshing?) and makes for a fun night.

The head table intros went well and their speeches, mercifully short, detailed the great work the police commission does for the Children's Hospital Foundation and other worthwhile causes plus, helping our head cop, Chief Jack Ewatski, launch his stand-up comic career.

He told how he enjoys reading to elementary school children and talking to them after, the most frequent question being: "How much do you make.?"

However, one little girl asked him: "Are those people you show as the most wanted really bad?"

"Very bad," the chief told her, "and my detectives are looking very hard for them."

"Well, if they're so bad" she said, "Why don't you just keep them when you're taking their picture?"

The meal, catered by the Fairmont Hotel, was, as usual, exceptional. There's a coupla new chefs there that are redefining the world of gastronomic delights! One chap at our table, with gray hair and glasses, actually begged for a second helping!

Then came The Winnipeg Police Pipe Band. Now I've heard them before and they're truly marvelous but this year they surpassed themselves! Their selections, clarity of tone and just their sheer artistry held me spellbound!

I'd be remiss if I didn't mention the live, Jay Harrison Big Band. The bands and their gifted vocalists in Winnipeg take a back seat to no one and these guys and gals were no exception. Fantastic!

Getting back to Parker and Ingebritsen, do you guys do Bar Mitzvahs?

June 16, 2002

FATHER'S DAY, 2002

We used to sit on the steps of our old house and he would muse about how well he remembered his early years and how tough it was to remember current things.

He would tell me about the orchards his family had in Russia. There were nut trees as well as fruit trees and he climbed them all!

He told me about his wild bird egg collection and the many adventures he had getting them, including one that involved climbing along the underside of an old bridge.

He told me about his Dad being a *"real live"* watchmaker and he would watch him for hours. Then when his Dad went on a trip he would sit at the bench and tinker with watches which outraged his father who wanted him to attend university.

His Dad would take their horse and buggy and visit the estates and castles in the surrounding area and examine and repair if necessary, all their timepieces. Once in a while he would go along and he loved it!

He told me how his granddad, nearly one hundred years old, would swim in the local lake. And how, at over a hundred years, he came into the house from a walk and called my Dad's parents over to his bed.

His granddad talked with them in quiet tones till his Mom started to cry. Then he asked the three kids to come over one by one and explained to them that he was about to die, gave them each a memento and then lay down on his bed and took his final sleep.

He disliked the taste of liquor but thought my Mom's cooking was food for the Gods!

He loved walking and could play cards with *the boys* all night long! He loved good music, and wouldn't miss the Metropolitan Opera radio broadcast every Saturday afternoon. He was a kind and gentle soul with a compassionate heart.

He taught me to love and respect Nature and all living things and how to dig a garden.

He was my Father, and I miss him.

November 10, 2002

BLESS 'EM ALL, BLESS 'EM ALL, THE YOUNG THE SHORT AND THE TALL...AND JOHN McCRAE

In Flanders field the poppies blow,
between the crosses, row on row,

Tomorrow is Remembrance Day but for me every day is remembrance day. For I enjoy life and living and I know full well that without the selfless sacrifice of those who did forgo the joy of making memories, I would not have had the freedom to make mine.

That make our place, and in the sky

The larks, still bravely singing fly,
Scarce heard amid the guns below.

The walks in the park that gladden me so much with different plants in bloom every time, treasures growing in the field or tucked away in unlikely pockets. And my playful dog Roxy making me roar with laughter as she tries to creep up on a squirrel!

And the multitude of birds and bugs, trees and sky and more wonders of creation which I have the freedom to savour.

We are the Dead. Short days ago
We lived, felt dawn, saw sunset glow,
Loved and were loved,
And now we lie in Flanders field.

I remember the awe of seeing my kite rise into the air and the bigger thrill when it climbed trying to reach the heavens or at least brush up against a cloud and kiss it.

And the extreme pleasure of being with my kids in the park yesterday and today and of course elsewhere (but the park is still the bestest place!) and I deeply ponder on those that perished that I might be so elated. We dare not ever forget.

Take up our quarrel with the foe.
To you from failing hands we throw the torch, be yours to hold it high.

The memories of family and friends floods my mind. They're gleeful and at times sad. But I realize I would have none of them if not for those who gave up living that I might experience life.

If ye break faith with us who die,
We shall not sleep,
Though poppies grow in Flanders field
How can we ever forget them, bless 'em all!

December 1, 2002

BIRTHDAYS, PAST AND PRESENT!

I've just recently attended my granddaughter Zoe's *Numero Uno* birthday party. The highlight for me and Zoe too, was when the birthday cake, all lit up, was brought into the living room.

After the candles were blown out with the help of the other kids at the party, Zoe attacked the cake with gusto 'cause Mommy said: "It's your cake, you can eat it!"

I got to thinkin' about birthdays and birthday cakes when I was a kid, you know, as my errant children describe the era, before electricity, phones or cars!

People would bake their own cakes then and carefully insert coins (usually pennies!) tightly wrapped in wax paper, with a dime, or a quarter, if you were in the chips, as the grand prize! It was terrific!

A further tradition at these events was serving *Paulin's Chocolate Puffs!* For those of you unfortunate enough not to have eaten these acne producers let me describe the process, 'cause you didn't just gulp 'em down, there was a process!

These gems consisted of four parts, the first part being the chocolate layer covering the marshmallow-like puff. Some portions came off in large flakes, others were more work, but worth it!

Secondly, you devoured the creamy puff underneath.

Thirdly, you licked, yes licked up the dollop of strawberry jam under the puff and finally you could eat the tasty chocolate-rimmed cookie under it all! Yummy!

I've heard it rumoured that my barely older brother Jerry, has maliciously contended that at one of my early birthday parties I took up a position near the front door under the guise of greeting my guests.

The story goes that if they didn't have a present with them, entry to the soiree was forbidden!

Those that know me give little credence to this tale, especially those that have grown up with a ruthless, older sibling.

His own birthday is in two days from this reading and I asked by dog Roxy what I should get him.

Having seen him stumble around of late, she suggested a walker. ***Happy Birthday buddy!***

January 12, 2003

OUR REMARKABLE ADVENTURE!

Starting this Thursday, we're having a grand re-opening FURNITURE GALLERY SALE!

We've come through a remarkable journey these past two years and have created for our clientele a shop without comparison or equal in Winnipeg and on a par with any, in Canada!

Where once we were the standard bearer for one major manufacturer, thus limiting our selection, we now carry several top quality lines giving our clientele an excellent and much wider variety of styles and price points. It's a remarkable world of choice in home furnishings heretofore unavailable in Winnipeg, ***ever!***

We still display in our distinctive room settings, only moreso(!) giving you an absolute ***virtual reality*** of seeing and examining our exciting and popular new lines "in play".

If you think we're just your Gramma's store, you better think again. We have many contemporary and fashion art styles that are retailing very well and our wealth of stunning accessories from around the world are sold throughout the continent and beyond!

Our designers and staff have done ***Yeoman's*** work in preparing our sales floor for the GRAND RE-OPENING of our furniture gallery.

It's very difficult for me giving these ladies such wonderful kudos 'cause I have a penchant for rather more acerbic remarks but their work is almost faultless and the results in a word, outstanding.

One small critique mind you comes from the boys in the back and our drivers. They've been lifting and pulling and tugging and pushing gorgeous and weighty pieces here and there not to mention hither and yon throughout our showroom helping in a major way to achieve this great look without much credit! So now you got credit, shut up already!

The only ***old thing*** still wandering the floor these days is me! In fact I heard ***Roxy***, my dog remark to one of the girls the other day that "... we should do something about the old fella..." Watch it ***Roxy!***

March 16, 2003

SPECTACULAR CHAIRS AND A BIT OF BLARNEY!

If you're askin' me about a wonderful Spring tonic not to mention a great chance to pick up a spectacular, one-of-a-kind accent chair, then this coming Friday, beginning at 7:00 p.m., you'd be better joinin' us at the Association for Community Living Manitoba Spring Chairity Auction, smack on the first floor of the Winnipeg Convention Centre.

The proceeds will assist the ACL in setting up group homes for mentally disabled individuals, giving them a chance to function in a more normal environment.

Initially, people contribute chairs no matter what shape they're in. They're brought into our warehouse and catalogued. Our guys do any small repairs or minor touch-ups.

We then contact designers, artists and other talented people to decorate them in such a manner as to fetch a goodly dollar at our annual CHAIRITY (not Charity!) Auction.

Talk about Cinderella, the make-overs are nothing short of sensational!

Last year's transformations were simply amazing!

This year, the results are nothing short of stupendous!

The artistry, imagination and just sheer talent available in our wonderful city is simply unbelievable! Wow!

So come by car, walk or run but don't miss this one, its a biggie!

There'll be a cash bar, finger food, draws, silent auction, the live auction and more.

Unfortunately my dog Roxy can't make it as she's got a bone to pick, (or is that chew?) with a Shih-Tzu.

And if you think I've used too much of the blarney just bless ya and be rememberin' that it's St. Patrick's Day tomorrow.

So I'll be after sayin' hello to my dear friend Paddy, gone but not forgotten, to the rest of the Twomeys and all the other great Irish families in our city, (especially those of us who wished we were!) here's me favorite Irish blessing ...

May the road rise up to meet you,
May the wind be always at your back,
May the sun shine warm upon your face,
May the rains fall soft upon your fields.
And until we meet again,
May God hold you in the palm of his hand.

From McRoxy and the O'Brick's!

March 23, 2003

SIMPLY A QUESTION OF SPACE!

When we moved from a small into a much larger house, we didn't know what to do with all the room.

We replaced our old claustrophobic bedroom closet with a lit walk-in one that had a large drawer chest to boot.

Getting out of bed didn't involve smacking the dresser with your knees and our bathroom was en suite!

The living/dining area was spacious and grand, super for parties not to mention a couple of weddings.

And besides a plethora of drawers our kitchen had room for a table the whole family could sit around!

Because I love gardening and really enjoy my yard, I'll probably be here forever.

But a lot of my customers who have winter homes and/or travel a lot and with the kids having flown the coop, decide to move into smaller premises.

Once you get over the shock that you can't take all your stuff with you, you got another one comin', lotta those old favorite furniture pieces don't fit, either the size or the new ambiance.

However, the furniture industry, in a bold move, laden with foresight, has designed furniture specially for Condominium Living!

While some Condos will be fairly large a number of people are looking for more compact sizes and there's lottsa furniture styles available!

For example, most of our sofa lines sport units that, while trimmer and more compact are, like furniture dealers, very chic.

There are occasional tables and lamps to complement these trimmer styles, some with multiple uses.

There's two piece dinettes perfect for kitchen snacks or more amply sized sets with matching chinas.

Or even a buffet only with a faux, Baker's Rack hutch.

Lots of newer bedroom items, while still occupying the usual floor space are much taller and hold a lot more goods.

I really can't move 'cause I'd have to train my wretchedly spoiled dog Roxy not to hog the entire sofa while I'm watching TV.

My son Stuart said I should mention that some of the trimmer scaled items would be ideal for those having purchased older, character homes, but I ain't got no room!

March 30, 2003

A BIG GUY, IN MANY WAYS!

The first time I really got a good glimpse of Nick Hill was at a Toronto Furniture show. We were approaching each other in a large aisle which he seemed to fill completely!

We nodded and he asked, "How's the show?!

"Found some good buys," I replied.

"Yep," he said as we smiled and passed each other. There was no bluster, no brashness. You could sense his measure, he was a big man and a straight shooter.

Over the years as I got to know him better, he only affirmed my original opinions.

I remember back in our early years, some Winnipeg furniture *mavens* predicted both our demises.

When the dust cleared a little while later and a lot of them were gone, Nick called. "You still there?"

"Yep," I said.

"Me too!" he chortled and we both laughed.

Besides being a character, a super good guy, a great salesman and so much more, he was also a *legend* in his time!

He was talked about with joviality, but also with reverence and respect. His commercials were a hoot, the TV ones almost costing me a lift home from the airport.

We'd arrived back from a furniture show and instead of just one, two of our kids showed up, each insisting we go with them. Suddenly, Nick appeared in the terminal. He'd come early and forgot to call ahead for a lift.

I tell him not to worry and ask my kids who wants to take Nick home.

Big mistake! They both do!

My brats are willing to abandon their parents for the thrill of taking Nick home!

One of my daughters explains, "He's on TV Dad! He's famous!"

The *loser* took us home.

When he wanted to bid for the Ashdown retail store on Main Street to house a furniture gallery, I wrote a laudatory letter. It was all true. Others did too but he wasn't successful. It was Winnipeg's loss! When my son Stuart heard of Nick's passing he remarked, "I guess The Guy upstairs said, "It's time for the *Come on Down* Guy to *Come On Up!*"

KING OF THE ~~MOUNTAIN~~ HILL

May 11, 2003

MEMORIES OF MOM

I was just a little kid, and my Mom was talking to me about her life as a child in Russia.

Though dreadfully poor, her family had bought her a new pair of shoes for the Passover.

She was ecstatic and wore them when she went to fetch something at a little distance. It rained on the way back and the shoes got dirty.

She stood by the side of the road and wept, eventually making her way home. Her Mother quickly cleaned them and comforted her.

To this day the story of that little girl crying in the rain tugs at my heart.

She was in elementary school in Winnipeg when her Mom died. As the eldest daughter she was pulled out of school to help raise her family, never finishing her education.

Most of her siblings left for the bright lights of New York when they were old enough, but she stayed to tend the remaining ones.

In her early thirties, after the last one left home, she traveled to New York to visit *her children*.

While there she was introduced to a strikingly handsome man whose wife had died leaving him with eleven-year-old twins.

After a whirlwind courtship, she married him and returned with him to Winnipeg to begin life as a new bride!

In the years that followed she had two children of her own.

Though life was tough we really didn't know we were needy 'cause everybody else was too! And besides she permeated our lives with love!

She was a fabulous cook. Her rice knishes and poppy seed cookies are legend in our family.

We ate good, healthy foods, her special vegetarian suppers being miles ahead of their time.

She swore she was over five feet tall and my brother Jerry and I, a couple of galoots, would stand beside her and agree, with silly grins on our faces.

Her memory evokes a kinder smile as we appreciate how tall she really was.

And by the way Mom, those twins you raised as your own are celebrating their eighty-third birthday today!

Happy Mother's Day

to all Mothers!

July 6, 2003

CUKES, TOMATOES, PEPPERS AND KIDS!

Years ago, fueled by a fire within, I elicited the unwilling help of my two older sons in turning a so-so back yard lawn into a lush garden replete with annual flowers and exotic roses. The assistance of the two older boys was obtained as they sought vainly to sneak out the side door to escape a couple of hours with spade or fork in hand, helping me dig up our clay based soil. One is now a gardener in his own right but the other had the audacity to escape to another city to do desk work and is only mentioned in muted tones at family suppers.

My youngest son, at that time just a toddler, escaped the physical rigours of gardening, instead using it as a place to play and run through with the sweet young thing from next door.

One year I was growing an unusually large cucumber called *Zeppelin*. On one vine, after a fruit had set, I stripped off the remaining flowers to let all the energy go into making one really big cuke. It started to grow quite large when Stu and his girlfriend came bounding and giggling through the garden.

I heard a crunch. The giggling stopped. I knew what had happened but I just kept on working. They soon ran by me and I thought, like the Blue Bombers (even then!), wait till next year!.

This young 'un now has a little garden of his own and he talks often about the performance of his cucumbers, tomatoes and especially his pepper plants, giving me visual measurements of his crop.

His daughter *Zoe*, an impish gem not yet two, plays in the yard while he gardens. Sound familiar?

Last week she brought him a gift, she'd picked the largest, unripe pepper and gave it to him.

Whatcha say? I asked. He said, "Thank you *Zoe*."

I thought back twenty plus years ago to a little guy and gal and a *Zeppelin* crunch and basked in a wonderful memory.

The acorn really doesn't fall too far from the tree!

FRUITS OF OUR LABOUR

August 31, 2003

A NIGHT AT THE OPERA (SORTA)!

When I saw Andrew Lloyd Webber's *Les Miserables*, all I got was a sore *tush*.

I couldn't remember any one song exciting enough to hum afterwards.

Cats was a bit different. The tune *Memories* was absolutely wonderful and almost, almost, carried the show. But once again I was plagued by the sore tush syndrome.

Don't Cry For Me Argentina, the lead song in *Evita,* was another fabulous number, but I was warned by many not to attend any performance, be it stage or movie.

So when Joseph and his coat came to Rainbow Stage, and I really enjoy Rainbow, I wasn't sure I'd attend. As a matter of fact I was so down on Andrew Lloyd Webber's offerings I was hardly tempted. However, a few sources in the know insisted I go, even without benefit of a soft cushion for Mon Tush!

Last Sunday, while walking at Kildonan Park in the early morning, I saw that this was the last night of Joseph. In a decision loaded with courage, bravery and daring I decided to give Andrew one more shot.

Wow! Despite Webber's operatic style, everything sung or chanted and lots of chorus commentary, the show was exceptional!

The male and female leads, I wish I knew their names, were outstanding. Their voices were rich and melodic and I could have listened to them all night!

And I know who played the Pharoah! Even though the voice was deeper and fuller, I knew that *Elvis* was alive and well in Winnipeg!

In a Pharoah's garb, replete with Blue Suede Shoes, this was one cool cat!

His eyes glistened with impish delight and his body writhed like a snake! I said he was cool!

Those Chamberlain dancers had nothing on this sexy cat!

However he did give me a problem, I had a hard time controlling the girls I was with!

My dog *Roxy* said it wasn't his performance, it was my own animal magnetism!

She really kids a lot. But I wonder...

September 7, 2003

COOLTV, IT'S COMIN'!

Thursday night at *CanWest Global's* headquarters in the Richardson Bldg. we attended the launch of, "**coolTV** the first channel in Canada entirely devoted to jazz in all its diversity."

When we got there around 6:00 the joint was abuzz with wall to wall people! Lots of Winnipeg's who's who including Conservative leader Stu Murray and Liberal leader Dr. Jon Gerrard.

After a few tête-à-têtes, a coupla drinks and some great hors d'oeuvre we left to continue celebrations at *Vertigo,* the Exchange District night-club in the building that formerly housed The Old Spaghetti Factory.

When we got there a trio was already in full swing and I thought I heard the late, great Louis Prima belting out a number!

The voice was a bit raspier and a bit deeper and simply great!

They played quite a few classics including *Moonglow, Blue skies* and ended with a request of an earlier number, the Duke Ellington classic, *It don't mean a thing if you ain't got that swing!*

Wow! It was not only great but impossible to keep your foot from tapping and your hands from clapping!

Again the bar was open and while the earlier hors d'oeuvre were grrreat, the offerings, including enough *Sushi* to satisfy even my daughters, at *Vertigo* were sensational! They had to be, just to keep in step with the music!

There was a break when the first group left for another gig and the second one started. The canned music in the interim fit the bill perfectly and we didn't even skip a beat!

The new group, consisting of reeds rather than strings, soon began playing and did a bang-up job keeping the ambiance alive and well!

And just in passing, I'm awe struck by the remarkable *Asper* family and their penchant for enriching our community, over and over, again!

When I got home I told my dog *Roxy,* who insists on knowing what's comin' down the pike, that there'd be a new TV channel specializing in cool Jazz.

Peering over her sunglasses, she said, "Would you expect less from the *Aspers?*"

For a dog, *Roxy's* one cool cat!

January 11, 2004

OH MY GOODNESS!

Being in furniture, I realize that if a space is narrow, furnish it with items light in scale and tone.

Unfortunately, though better than previous years, my "too narrow" greenhouse, has again become a crowded jungle!

The most severe problem, besides knocking everything over in a simple walk down the aisle, is trying to water the flora.

Plants on shelves are OK; the hanging ones, a nightmare! Water gets all over the place amidst much mumbling, cursing (for shame!) and babbling!

However, I've developed a unique watering method for The *Hanging Gardens of BabbleLand!!*

I attach a bungee cord to the hanging basket hook and re-hang it suspended on the bungee cord.

Next, please follow this carefully, it's very clever! I place a large planting bowl directly under the hanging plant now suspended at a low, much easier to reach level. Watering lowers the plant even more making it easy to water heavily. It drains freely into the bowl underneath sounding like torrential rain! Well, noisy anyway!

I was about to start this process one afternoon when I discovered I had company in the greenhouse. *Zoe,* my two year old plus granddaughter had snuck in and before touching everything she could lay her hands on, she gave me an irresistable impish grin.

Hooked again, I beckoned her over. I said, "We're gonna water plants and you gotta help me."

She looked at me strange. I swear she was thinking, "Does he really know what he's doing?"

After much amusing chatter and odd noises to keep her attention, the process started.

The water from the watering can descended upon the plant in a fantastic, cascading deluge hitting the catch bowl below with a raucous rush! (Wow, this is Pulitzer stuff!)

Zoe's eyes got as wide as saucers! I added two more containers of water. It was smashing. I've always liked the sound, but it was more better through *Zoe's* eyes!

Suddenly, this gorgeous little imp, with arms askew, shouted, "*Oh my goodness! Oh my goodness!*"

My dog Roxy looked up and said, "You're lucky she didn't use one of your expressions *Gramps!*"

"Amen" I said.

February 22, 2004

TALKING BOOKS

Since my eyes decided to weaken, making it somewhat difficult for me to read books, magazines or even the newspaper, I've been literally starved for the written word! I used to be a voracious reader, at times having several books going at once. Besides novels, true adventure tales, and mysteries, I read a great number of garden books, magazines and some political tracts, just so I could try to grasp what manner of discipline our politicians were now spouting! And wouldn't you know it, no matter where I went some smart chick would come up and say "Have you read *The Client*?" or some other novel by this *Chisholm* chap. "The Client" I would murmur and it soon became apparent that I wasn't reading anything popular. Even my son, who has a difficult time getting past the hockey scores, read The Client. I just had to find a way to "read" again, I did! I discovered *Audio Books* at our public libraries. Then I found someone with a car, desperate enough for lunch and liquor to take me. I first tried out the system with some old favorites and found the secret to audio reading was staying awake! This is no mean trick! You lie down usually at night, turn on your cassette player and some smooth talking person is reading to you. If you ain't concentrating real good, you're gone! The most popular key on my cassette became *rewind*, as I had to go back several times before I finished a track. But I got it! Then I started with the contemporary stuff and I've already read about eight Chisholm novels including The Client!. So the next time I braved a cocktail party I went up to a group of women, and in a somewhat haughty manner asked, "Have you read Chisholm's new book, The Summons or his homespun effort, The Painted House?" "By who" They chorused. "Chisholm, you know, John Chisholm. He wrote, The Client." I grinned with a superior air. "You mean, *Grisham, John Grisham*." "Uh, yeah", I muttered, "Just testing you." But they knew. The women always know. I heard snickers as I skulked away. The next day when I wanted to take my dog *Roxy* for a walk she said, "Love to Dad, but let's just wait till this *Grisham - Chisholm* thing blows over." Bad news travels fast.

and then she said..
..you can't imagine..

March 21, 2004

ZOE, ZAIDA AND WOXY

A while back my son Stuart with wife Steph and daughter Zoe bought a house near me.

It needed some work before they could move in and I suggested they move in with me to save rent and have a built-in baby sitter.

They were here near four months in which time Steph taught me that you can wash clothes in cold water, Stu, that my car was designed to carry hockey sticks, and Zoe, that leaving my bedroom door open was an invitation for exploration.

I remember telling Steph one day that one of my Audio books was missing.

"Where'd you leave it?" she asked.

"On my night table.

"That's the first place she'd look!" she said. Zoe's parents fussed over her, read to her, talked to her and corrected her by explaining why she shouldn't do what she was doin'.

I thought this a sure-fire recipe for spoiling the kid! It didn't happen.

Still, she'd drive me wacky, taking stuff outta my room. I once complained to Stu about something I was sure Zoe had taken. He said, "Ask her." I said, "Zoe," where's my TV remote?" She marched into her room and said, "Here *Zaida*," retrieving it from under her bed. That day I realized how much I'd come to love that little imp.

I have four other wonderful grandchildren - Jonathon, Paula, Aliya, and Daniel who also call me *Zaida*, Yiddish for Grampa, but I've always felt too young to be a *Zaida*.

However, being so close to the love of this little vixen, *Zaida* became a delightful word! "Hi *Zaida!*" in the morning became the cheeriest sound of my day!

"That's my *Zaida!*" when she'd spot me at her uncle Ira's Deli made my heart flutter!

And, "G'night Zaida." at bedtime gave me joy and inner peace.

She called my dog *Roxy*, "*Woxy*" and I could eat her up!

When she left for the first night to sleep in her new house I sat in my chair and gazed at the door.

Roxy came up and nestled her head under my hand. "I love her too", she said.

I know *Woxy*, I know...

G'night Zaida
G'night
Woxy

Zzzz
Zzzzz

THE END